CUBAN MIAMI

Cuban Miami

ROBERT M. LEVINE AND MOISÉS ASÍS

RUTGERS UNIVERSITY PRESS   NEW BRUNSWICK, NEW JERSEY, AND LONDON

Library of Congress Cataloging-in-Publication Data

Levine, Robert M.

   Cuban Miami / by Robert M. Levine and Moisés Asís.

     p. cm.

   Includes bibliographical references.

   ISBN 0–8135–2780–5 (cloth : alk. paper)

    1. Cuban Americans—Florida—Miami Region—History—20th century—Pictorial works. 2. Exiles—Florida—Miami Region—History—20th century—Pictorial works. 3. Political refugees—Florida—Miami Region—History—20th century—Pictorial works. 4. Miami Region (Fla.)—Emigration and immigration—History—20th century—Pictorial works. 5. Cuba—Emigration and immigration—History—20th century—Pictorial works. I. Title. II. Asís, Moisés, 1952–

F319.M6 L48 2000

975.9'381004687291 21—dc21

                                     99–045919

British Cataloging-in-Publication data for this book is available from the British Library

Book design and composition by Jenny Dossin

Manufactured in the United States of America

To all exiles and immigrants whose journey is difficult

CONTENTS

W E WISH TO EXPRESS our appreciation to those who offered help: Norbert Adler, Eladio Alfonso, Mariela C. Alvarez, Teresa and Dina Asís, Bernardo Benes, Marta Berros, Sam Boldrick, Luis J. and Aurora Botifoll, Juan Campos A., Barry Carr, Alejandro "Alex" Cruz, Leslie Cyphen, Rafael and Jorgelina Díaz, Lincoln Díaz-Balart, Juan Carlos Espinosa, M. Roberto Fernández, Jeremy Gates, Lissette González, Lidia González-Prada, Adela Herrera, Dawn Hughes, Diana González Kirby, Michael LaRosa, Max Lesnick, Adolfo Leyva, Pablo I. López, Mary Lorenzo, Natalie B. Lyons, Rafael C. Marqués, Alfred Mason, Gustavo J. Miyares, Pedro S. Osorio, Alex Penelas, Demetrio Pérez Jr., Ernesto Pichardo, Ileana Ros-Lehtinen, George Sánchez, Peter Sánchez, Ricardo and Vivian Sánchez, José Enrique Souto, José M. Szapocznik, José and Dulce Valera, Esperanza B. de Varona, and Bryan O. Walsh. Special thanks go to José M. Varela, who drew cartoons especially for the book, and to Patricia García-Vélez, who helped us as part of her University of Miami Honors Program summer research project.

Cuban Miami traces the history of the Cuban American community in the Greater Miami area, especially its human dimension—the effect of exile on hundreds of thousands of Cubans, and their effect on Miami. In keeping with the Rutgers University Press series in which it is the second volume, *Cuban Miami* offers that history through imagery as well as text. We hope that it captures the texture and spirit of the city's Cuban American community.

CUBAN MIAMI

Lisset Vera symbolizes Cuba in bondage at the 122d anniversary of José Martí's birth, January 28, 1975. PHOTO: HISTORICAL MUSEUM OF SOUTHERN FLORIDA

Preserving *Cubanidad*

Cuban americans call Miami the "Exile Capital." You can find there, for instance, more Cuban restaurants, cafeterias, bakeries, coffee counters, and food wagons than in Cuba itself. The city lies across the Straits of Florida from the alligator-shaped island only 198 miles from Havana—156 miles closer than Florida's capital, Tallahassee.

Look at a map of the Gulf of Mexico, where the Atlantic meets the Caribbean Sea. South and east of the Florida Keys, Cuba stretches 750 miles east to west, the distance from New York to Chicago. Dominating the western Antilles, the island is dotted with scores of natural harbors along its northern coast that make departures by ship easy, especially when weather conditions cooperate.

No wonder, then, that for two hundred years, Cuban exiles have chosen to emigrate to the United States, and especially to Florida. During Cuba's struggle for independence (1868–1898), as many as one-tenth of all Cubans took refuge in U.S. cities, including Key West, Tampa, and New York. Cuba and Florida have always been linked, not only geographically but economically. North American investments in Cuba reached $50 million at the close of the nineteenth century and $1.3 billion by the 1920s.[1] "By the mid-twentieth century," notes Louis A. Pérez Jr., "Cuba operated almost entirely within the framework of the economic system of the United States." Yet the total number of Cuban-born residents in the United States before the late 1950s was modest, probably fewer than twenty thousand.

Then, in 1959, Fidel Castro's victory over Cuba's dictator Fulgencio Batista triggered an exodus of more than 665,000 Cubans to Miami. A first wave of exiles arrived between 1959 and 1961, a second between 1961 and 1977. In 1980, a third wave of 124,776 Cubans came by sea via the Mariel boat lift, and tens of thousands have made the journey since—the fortunate in planes and boats, the desperate less fortunate in rafts.[2]

"History of Cuban Exile" by José M. Varela. (1) In the remote past, Cubans arrived at the Florida wilderness. (2) And they founded Miami . . . . (4) They brought with them strange rites, like Santería and "exile nostalgia." (5) Each wave came with an exotic name ("worm," "marielito," "rafter," "dissident"). (8) But according to prophecies on the radio, . . . the last exile has yet to arrive.

Between 1960 and 1980, at least a million Cubans emigrated—10 percent of the island's population.[3] Of these, 85 percent fled to Puerto Rico or to the U.S. mainland. Some settled in far-off locations such as Chicago, Los Angeles, and, especially, Union City, New Jersey, which in the 1960s and 1970s became known as "Havana on the Hudson"; by 1975, two-thirds of the city's people were Cuban. Yet by the 1990s, many of Union City's older residents had moved to Florida. Many others relocated throughout the Northeast.[4]

Some Cuban exiles have moved as far from their homeland as Spain and Australia (where today the Cuban community numbers between two and three thousand), and, closer to home, to Venezuela and Argentina, as well as Puerto Rico. In 1994, the Spanish newspaper *Cambio* reported that more than a million and a half Cubans had fled the island and Castro's brand of socialism en route to twenty-five different countries.[5]

But it was to Miami that the exiles came in overwhelming numbers, and they found a city—in fact, the whole of South Florida—ripe for development. The Cubans transformed not only their populations but their landscapes, their economies, and their cultures. What the Cubans achieved in Miami, Cuban American banker Luis J. Botifoll believes, could not have happened if they had concentrated in New York or Atlanta or some other already dynamic city.[6]

Only in Miami, the center of *el exilio*, the Cuban exodus, would the Cuban exiles prosper so, economically and politically. Many incoming Cubans were highly educated and business-wise. In just over two years after Castro's takeover, for example, in March 1961, aides to President John F. Kennedy's Health, Education, and Welfare secretary Abraham Ribicoff estimated that three-fourths of the faculty of the University of Havana were living in South Florida.

By the late 1970s, Cuban Americans had become the wealthiest group of

Hispanic origin in the United States, surpassing in economic power all other Latino communities around the country. And by the mid-1990s, Cuba's need for funds remitted from abroad—a large percentage of which came from Cuban Americans—had become so acute that the official party line changed from tarring the refugees as traitors to dubbing them with the milder "economic immigrants."[7]

As new Americans, the exiles, like immigrant groups, faced barriers and problems in their adopted country. Their behavioral values conflicted with those they found in the United States. Many Cuban Americans in South Florida today, like immigrants from other Latin American countries, have preserved their cultural identity (*cubanidad*) by honoring at least some traditions from their home country—in this case, the Spanish language, and, for most community members, the Roman Catholic faith.

Cultural barriers sometimes affected women more than men: Parents expected their daughters, for example, to live at home until they were married, although young "Anglo" women routinely went away to college, took jobs in other cities, and otherwise declared their independence. Economic barriers loomed large for exiles who could not speak fluent English or lacked specific training or who were barred from their professions because their Cuban licenses would not transfer. Discrimination raised a third kind of barrier, especially for Cubans of Asian or African background.

Some (and sometimes all) of these obstacles translated for many exiles into low self-esteem, isolation, and cultural confusion.[8]

On the whole, however, Cuban Americans found ways around these obstacles much more skillfully than have most other new arrivals. They built a strong social and political community and fitted themselves comfortably into a foreign culture, while maintaining a good portion of what they had brought with them in their hearts, if not in their suitcases.

Old Miami

ALL FLORIDA SCHOOLCHILDREN learn that, at one time or another, five flags have flown over their state: the flags of Spain (twice), Britain, the United States, and the Confederacy.

When Columbus's three ships crossed the Atlantic in 1492, several hundred thousand indigenous people inhabited present-day North Florida and southern Georgia. About a decade later, a shipwrecked Basque sailor washed up at what is now known as the Miami River at Biscayne Bay, the wide expanse of water that lies north of the Keys. In 1513, Juan Ponce de León—looking for

First afternoon tea at the clubhouse in Lummus Park, at North River Drive and Northwest 2d Street, 1893. The park lay near the terminus of Henry Flagler's East Coast Railroad, opened in 1896. Miami also incorporated as a city that year and established its first public schools, one for whites and the other for blacks. PHOTO BY HOIT; ROMER COLLECTION, MIAMI-DADE PUBLIC LIBRARY

Fox hunt on the grounds of the Biltmore Hotel, Coral Gables, circa 1924. Today a fashionable resort surrounded by Spanish-style homes and a golf course, the Biltmore failed during the Depression, became a military hospital during World War II, and reopened in the 1980s. PHOTO: UNIVERSITY OF MIAMI SPECIAL COLLECTIONS

the fabled Fountain of Youth—made a more deliberate visit to Biscayne Bay, which he called "Chequescha" in his diary (his understanding of the name of the local Tequesta people). Eight years later, he returned, sailing from Cuba with a large naval force to conquer Florida. Ponce de León was wounded in the failed invasion, and he was taken back to Cuba, where he died.

The Spanish crown ruled the region for most of the years between 1513 and 1821, administering Cuba and Florida jointly from Havana. On many sixteenth-century maps, the two appear as a single land mass. By 1566,

Palm Pharmacy and Sunoco gas station, Hialeah, 1925. Miami's mid-twenties real estate frenzy later extended to Hialeah, an incorporated town near Miami. Decades later, the area would become more than 90 percent Hispanic. PHOTO: ROMER COLLECTION, MIAMI-DADE PUBLIC LIBRARY

Aerial view of Hialeah, 1925. The town was developed by Glenn Curtiss, who had made a fortune designing airplanes. Hialeah's handsome racetrack, with flamingos imported from Cuba, became a leading tourist attraction when it opened in 1932—although the flamingos escaped and flew back to the island. PHOTO: ROMER COLLECTION, MIAMI-DADE PUBLIC LIBRARY

The Ku Klux Klan in Miami's Fiesta of the American Tropics parade, 1926. During the 1920s, the nativist and bigoted Klan thrived all across Florida. In South Florida, the group was especially strong in Homestead, Davie, and a Miami much more "southern" than it is today. Photo: Romer Collection, Miami-Dade Public Library

Bathing beauties, 1926, part of the glamour of life under the South Florida sun touted to investors. But the real estate boom peaked the year this photo was taken. A ship foundered in Miami harbor and blocked shipping for several weeks, and, on September 17 and 18, a hurricane struck the city and 144 people perished. Photo: Romer Collection, Miami-Dade Public Library

Members of the Seminole tribe shoot arrows toward the setting sun in a ceremony held in the Everglades a few miles west of Miami, February 5, 1927. The Seminoles lived in palmetto-thatched structures and were tolerated unless they got in the way of the city's growth. Photo: Romer Collection, Miami-Dade Public Library

First National Bank, downtown Miami, 1929. Miami was a "wide-open" city during the waning years of Prohibition, when many profited from gambling and liquor smuggling. PHOTO: ROMER COLLECTION, MIAMI-DADE PUBLIC LIBRARY

Spanish priests had started to establish missions in the north and west of the peninsula. They proposed to convert the Kalulusa (or Calusa), who had lived on the land for two thousand years, to Catholicism.[1] The priests also established a mission, which they called Tequesta, on the Miami River. Several years later, with the natives complaining of abuse from the Spaniards, the mission was abandoned. By the mid-1700s, fewer than a hundred indigenous people remained on the Florida peninsula.

Visiting Cuban postal officials in front of a tri-motor plane at Miami's Pan American Airways terminal, Coconut Grove, 1930. Many visitors flew between Havana and Miami, and the first exiled Cubans, including ex-president Mario García Menocal and ex-dictator Gerardo Machado, arrived in the city by plane. Photo: Romer Collection, Miami-Dade Public Library

Pan American Airways terminal, Coconut Grove, circa 1930. A boy flown from Havana for medical treatment is carried by stretcher from the seaplane. Photo: Romer Collection, Miami-Dade Public Library

Britain seized Havana in 1762, then traded Cuba to Spain in exchange for Florida. When Spain regained control of Florida twenty-one years later, some of the Spanish Floridians who had fled to Cuba returned, many to St. Augustine, several hundred miles up the east coast of the peninsula from Miami.

Riverside Elementary students march in front of the Royal Club on West Flagler Street, circa 1932. The school served the neighborhood that in the early 1960s would become Little Havana. PHOTO: UNIVERSITY OF MIAMI SPECIAL COLLECTIONS

"Anglo" Riverside Elementary students, 1933. PHOTO: ROMER COLLECTION, MIAMI-DADE PUBLIC LIBRARY

Promotional photograph, Miami Beach, 1933. Developed by hotelier Carl Fisher, Miami Beach attracted wealthy winter vacationers from the North with polo, pari-mutual betting, and speedboat racing. Fisher excluded Jews and blacks from the Beach's hotels and private clubs. Photo: Romer Collection, Miami-Dade Public Library

A MIAMI SUNDAE

◆ Take a generous portion of the golden sun-kissed sands of Miami Beach, add several splashes of emerald green sea waves tempered with the warm, blue water of the Gulf Stream, sprinkle with the feathery shadows of wind-blown palm fronds, top off with puffs of white and gold billowy clouds, and serve out of doors with a background of tropical blooms and melodies of song-birds.

Photo and Text
Copyrighted by G. W. Romer
1933

Tahiti Beach, Coral Gables, 1933. Miami was a haven for nudists and natural healing cults. The largest nudist camp, the Spirit of the Palm, dated from the early 1920s. Photo: Romer Collection, Miami-Dade Public Library

Between the Revolutionary War and 1819, Florida became a haven for runaways and invaders: British Tories fleeing south from the American colonies, smugglers, and slaves from the Deep South, 250 of whom were murdered by Andrew Jackson's troops.

In 1821 the U.S. government formally annexed Florida, then reneged on its promise to compensate the Spanish crown for the land. Escaped slaves were captured and sold back into slavery, and Spanish subjects were permitted to depart for Cuba, where royal officials gave each arriving family land and a black bondsman.[2] Five years later, as the United States prepared to go to war against the Seminoles, federal soldiers built Fort Dallas at the entrance to Biscayne Bay. In 1845, when Florida became the twenty-seventh state in the Union, South Florida (except for Key West) remained a land of malarial swamps.

In Cuba, 1868 marked the beginning of a thirty-year struggle for independence from Spain. In its final years, José Martí led a revolution that wrested from Spain all of Cuba but the major coastal cities. Meanwhile,

Outdoor laundering, 1934. Most blacks lived in Colored Town (later known as Overtown); all black children attended segregated schools. Mercedes H. Byron, an African American writer, identified two Miamis in 1942: "Mi-ami and Their-ami." PHOTO: ROMER COLLECTION, MIAMI-DADE PUBLIC LIBRARY

hundreds of Cubans fled to the United States, where they founded exile communities in Key West, Tampa, Jacksonville, New York, and New Orleans. Workers from Cuba, hired by the season, signed contracts to make cigars in Tampa and Ybor City.[3] With Cuba's independence in 1902, most natives who had fled Spanish Cuba returned to the island. Some who remained founded Marti City in central Florida, later renamed Ocala.[4]

Not until 1870 did the first U.S. settlers arrive in the Biscayne Bay area. In 1896, Miami, now connected with the North by Henry Flagler's railroad, was incorporated as a city. During World War I, tourist hotels opened for business and a bridge went up to connect the city to Miami Beach. After the war, hundreds of thousands of land speculators rushed to the state, where 25,000 real estate agents happily took their money. A severe hurricane that struck South Florida in September 1926 was followed by an economic depression that foreshadowed the Wall Street crash by two years.

Miami—nearby, and easy to reach by plane or boat—continued to draw Cubans. Though their island enjoyed one of the highest per-capita living

Former Cuban dictator Gerardo Machado in exile in Miami, circa 1934. Machado, who died on March 30, 1939, was buried in the city's Woodlawn Memorial Cemetery. Photo: University of Miami Special Collections

Hotel Villa D'Este, center, with Daily News Tower in background, Biscayne Boulevard, 1941. The hotel was a favorite of visitors from Spain and Latin America, especially Cuba. In 1947, *Newsweek* reported, Cubans spent more than $70 million in Florida, where vacations in Miami were much cheaper than at Varadero Beach on the island.

standards in Latin America, a small but steady trickle of emigrés crossed the straits to South Florida, many seeking to escape poverty, others running from the authoritarian regimes of Gerardo Machado and Fulgencio Batista.[5] (Machado and Batista themselves would eventually become exiles, along with many other pre-Castro Cuban political figures.)

Unlike some Latin Americans, Cubans appreciated U.S. culture, and many affluent families had routinely sent their children to school in the

Shops on Northwest Twelfth Avenue north of West Flagler Street, circa 1950. Miami's postwar boom was fueled by the return of veterans who wanted to live in the city where they had been stationed while in training. PHOTO: ROMER COLLECTION, MIAMI-DADE PUBLIC LIBRARY

Riverside, 1956. By 1960, Cuban families would begin to move into the neighborhood that would evolve into Little Havana. Within a decade, Spanish-language signs would replace many of those in English in the fifties. PHOTO: HISTORICAL MUSEUM OF SOUTHERN FLORIDA

United States. The University of Miami in nearby Coral Gables, much closer to Cuba than to Gainesville, the home of the University of Florida, played the University of Havana in football in the 1920s and 1930s and recruited students from the best Cuban secondary schools. In 1950, 15 percent of the students at Miami's Barry College, a Catholic college for women, were Latin American, an unusually large percentage for a U.S. college at that time. And most of Barry's Latin students were Cuban.

Cubana Airlines advertisement from the *Griffin Guide to Greater Miami*, 1956. While Americans in the 1950s were traveling to Cuba to gamble and enjoy Havana's famous nightlife, Cubans were visiting Miami to shop and sightsee. Air conditioning was becoming more widespread, and the city seemed ready for growth. Some shops hung "Se habla español" signs to attract Cuban tourists.

PHOTO: UNIVERSITY OF MIAMI SPECIAL COLLECTIONS

By 1952, with its palm trees and pseudo-Spanish-style architecture and miles of beaches and waterfront, Miami was a sprawling, subtropical tourist's town. In the city proper lived 247,262 people, a number that doubled when one counted the surrounding metropolitan area of Dade County, which stretched south to the entrance to the Keys. World War II vets who had trained in South Florida came back to start businesses or to take advantage of the GI Bill. Fleets of National and Pan American propeller-driven DC-6s ferried in northeasterners eager to warm themselves under South Florida's sun. Most homes still relied on ceiling fans to combat the heat and humidity, although some had sprouted room air conditioners in their windows.

As much a part of South Florida as bougainvillea and sport fishing, discrimination—democratically applied to all minorities—held sway in many of the fashionable hotels and resorts in postwar Miami and Miami Beach, and in neighboring Coral Gables and Hialeah. African Americans, who lived north of downtown or in the far south of the county, worked as servants and laborers and sat in the back of the bus. Miami in 1952 had fifty-six elementary schools for whites and thirteen for "colored." Where permitted, Jews settled in Miami Beach and near Southwest 8th Street, leading out of town. Roman Catholics remained a small minority.

Now, in the mid-1950s, exiled Cuban politicians in Miami hatched plots and conspiracies against the Batista dictatorship. At Miami Beach's Lucerne Hotel and in his home in South Miami, the ousted Cuban president Carlos Prío Socarrás financed conspirators. One of his visitors was young Fidel Castro, who had spent two years in one of Batista's prisons after he led an unsuccessful armed attack on a Santiago de Cuba army barracks on July 26, 1953. Prío contributed money to the ongoing rebellion. With such donations, Castro bought the fifty-eight-foot yacht *Granma*, which he landed, filled with rebels, in Cuba's Oriente province in December 1956.[6]

Daily News Tower, circa 1963. This building was soon to become known as the Freedom Tower because of the social assistance programs housed in it for arriving Cubans. PHOTO: CELIA NÚÑEZ FERNÁNDEZ FAMILY

By 1958, only about 10,000 Cubans lived in Miami: 3,500 residents and the rest mostly young people fleeing Batista. A number of the city's shops and hotels catered to Latin American visitors. Affluent Cubans flew in fifty-five minutes from Havana to Coconut Grove's Dinner Key terminal, perhaps shopped at Burdine's department store and lunched at La Rumba, and flew home. The Cuban government operated a tourist office on Flagler Street, managed by Dolores Rey Morán. Miami's Tourist Board published brochures in Spanish and Portuguese. In downtown Miami, the Hotel America, owned by Miguel Oubrocq, advertised in Spanish and promised that it was "near Hispanic churches, shops, and restaurants." La Rumba imported Miami's first Cuban coffee machine. The Hotel Villa d'Este advertised single rooms for three dollars and doubles starting at five dollars in "el hotel en Miami de los latinoamericanos."

On Miami Beach, Dunhill's Ambassador Cafeteria announced that it had a "Gerente Cubano" (Cuban manager), Alfredo Alonso. Young Spanish-speaking women worked for hotels (including the Hotel Patricia on Southeast Second Avenue and the Hotel Miami Colonial, which faced Bayfront Park) as personal shoppers, happy to squire visitors to the finest shops. Hispanic tourists who overate or suffered other travelers' ailments had a choice of four physicians with Spanish surnames who advertised in tourist magazines.[7]

On January 1, 1959, as Batista fled Havana not far ahead of Castro's *barbudos* (bearded ones), Greater Miami was home almost exclusively to white southerners (who pronounced the city's name Myam'uh), retired Jews and Italians from New York, and blacks, including some Bahamians. Outside the city lay scrub land and strawberry and tomato farms. Tampa, with its cigar factories, had more Hispanics.

The Politics of Dislocation

A<small>NTI-BATISTA</small> C<small>UBANS</small> in Miami rejoiced when Fidel Castro took over Cuba in January 1959, an event that did not make the front page of the *Miami Herald*. Many made plans to end their exile. But in Cuba, patriots who had fought or sympathized with the self-pronounced "Maximum Leader" soon had misgivings. Castro lashed out at those who challenged his policies, purging his own supporters as ruthlessly as he persecuted former Batista officials. Castro's "revolutionary justice" included a judicial system bullied into overturning verdicts of acquittal for Batista sympathizers. In the space of a few months, the revolution's new prime minister, José Miró Cardona, and its new president, Manuel Urrutia, resigned.

Castro's reforms raised working-class wages, lowered working-class rents, and seized the assets of the well-to-do. Within two years, new laws had nationalized all large tracts of agricultural land. All sugar factories became the property of Cuba. According to the second most powerful figure in the new government, Ernesto Che Guevara, "The people want revolution first and elections later."[1] No elections were held.

Before the year was up, nearly thirty-five thousand of "the people" had left the island. The first to leave were those who feared they would be arrested or imprisoned, especially officials of Batista's police, armed forces, and government. (Anticipating disaster, some in these positions had fled in 1958.) Landowners, industrialists, managers, and other employees of expropriated businesses, as well as revolutionaries who had opposed Batista but now saw themselves and the revolution as betrayed, became personae non grata. Almost all of the exiled were highly educated, among them Cuba's most skillful technicians and administrators, and most of them came to Miami.

Some Cubans who left before Castro took over—many high government officials and the financial elite—had managed to transfer generous sums of money to established accounts in the United States. Even without foreign accounts, a Cuban businessman in Miami confided, "there were ways to take out money."[2] As the months passed, though, these transfers became next to impossible. Cubans who brought pesos out with them found that the island's 1:1 exchange rate did not apply elsewhere. And when Castro issued new currency, their old pesos proved as worthless as czarist bonds or Confederate dollars.

By 1961, Cubans who wanted to emigrate had begun to run into serious difficulties. Airline tickets had to be purchased in dollars. At airports, exiles were harassed as their papers were processed by mean-spirited militiamen, who sometimes subjected departing passengers to strip searches. The Cuban press ridiculed the exiles, calling them *gusanos* (worms). Young men of army age were detained in Cuba.[3] The Castro government allowed Cubans whom they did permit to go to carry only five dollars in cash and a suitcase; their property in Cuba was immediately confiscated. Nothing stanched the flow of emigrés.

Cubans who left in this first wave, between 1959 and 1962, were mostly white and affluent. In Miami they found a city in economic recession— most jobs available to them were menial. Cubans who had been profession- als were blocked from practicing in the United States until they passed qualifying examinations, which for many meant first acquiring sufficient English skills to do so. For several years, angry exiles who had been attorneys in Cuba picketed the Florida Bar Association for its refusal to administer the bar examination in Spanish. Many Cuban physicians went to work as hos- pital orderlies or lab technicians.

When the exiles in their dramatic numbers overloaded Miami's public resources, private charities stepped in with housing, relief, and jobs. Until late 1960, Dade County schools accepted exile children, who were not per-

manent residents, only if their families paid tuition, so the Catholic archdiocese hired Cuban teachers and took the children without charge into its
parochial schools. The Church petitioned Florida's state government for
help, without success.[4] Headed by Monsignor Bryan O. Walsh, the Irish-
born director of Miami's Catholic Welfare Bureau, volunteers worked
around the clock to accommodate the exiles. When Walsh's efforts led to the
passage, in January 1961, of the Cuban Refugee Assistance Program, federal
funds allotted each Cuban exile family $100 a month, reimbursed Jackson
Memorial Hospital for exiles' health care, and made college loans available
to exile students. Under the administration of Dwight D. Eisenhower and in
expanded form under John F. Kennedy's, the program gave unprecedented
levels of support to the exiles.

But that came later. In December 1960, James Baker, the headmaster of
Havana's elite Ruston Academy, asked Miami's archdiocese for help getting
children out of Cuba. The result was the Peter (or Pedro) Pan airlift.[5] Father
Walsh helped arrange the initial flight of two hundred children from
Havana to Miami. After Havana's U.S. Embassy closed, Penny Powers, a

Dr. Manuel Artime, who headed
Miami's Movimiento de Recuperación
Revolucionaria, was an exiled anti-Batista
guerrilla officer. The civilian chief of
Brigade 2506, he was captured in the Bay
of Pigs invasion. PHOTO: CELIA NÚÑEZ
FERNÁNDEZ FAMILY

British nurse who had helped evacuate Jewish children from Germany to London, took over the Cuban end of the operation, which at the beginning was kept secret. Relatives of former Cuban president Ramón Grau San Martín pitched in, along with staff members from various European embassies in Havana. Among other strategies, they sometimes falsified passports to evacuate youths of military age who would have been forced to remain.

Brigade 2506 veterans in Havana before their release in exchange for food and medical supplies, December 1962. After the Kennedy administration's last-hour refusal to support the Bay of Pigs invasion, Cuban exiles realized that no return to Cuba would occur in the near future. Their efforts shifted to improving their economic situation as Miami residents. PHOTO: HISTORICAL MUSEUM OF SOUTHERN FLORIDA

Women activists awaiting the return of anti-Castro commandos arrested in Nassau, Bahamas, their base for a planned infiltration of Cuba. PHOTO: CELIA NÚÑEZ FERNÁNDEZ FAMILY

That the Pedro Pan flights were permitted at all amounted to a kind of miracle. Once in the United States, the children moved in with foster families in Miami and elsewhere until their families could join them. When the operation ran out of temporary families, the Miami diocese set up five

Pedro Pan boys outside the Jesuit Boy's Residence in Miami, 1963. As adults three decades later, some Pedro Pan exiles expressed gratitude for their rescue, while others felt bitter over mistreatment they recalled. Some complained about their foster home placements and long separations from their families. PHOTO: UNIVERSITY OF MIAMI SPECIAL COLLECTIONS

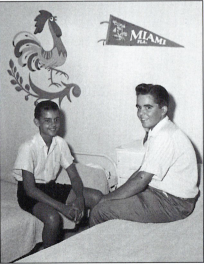

Pedro Pan roommates at the Florida City shelter, near the Everglades, 1963. PHOTO: UNIVERSITY OF MIAMI SPECIAL COLLECTIONS

camps around South Florida: Matecumbe (later renamed Boys' Town), Florida City, Kendall, Jesuit Boy's Home, and St. Raphael. Not all the young people's accommodations were ideal. Matecumbe, near the Everglades, was isolated, and children cried themselves to sleep. Mistreatment was reported in some facilities.

Yet Pedro Pan succeeded overall. In December 1960 and throughout 1961, the airlift brought 14,048 minors from Cuba to the United States. Some would later become well known locally: radio newsman and Miami city commissioner Tomás Regalado, Miami Chamber of Commerce president Armando Codina, singer Willy Chirino, businessman José Badia, and Miami mayor Joe Carollo.

For their part in organizing the airlift, Ramón and Polita Agüero Grau, the nephew and niece of former president Ramón Grau, were imprisoned for years by Cuban State Security Police. Polita Grau was held for fourteen years in a women's prison under harrowing conditions. Prisoners who sympathized with hunger strikers, for example, were savagely beaten and locked in dark cells for months. Ramón Grau spent twenty-three years in prison.

Once in the United States, new arrivals from Cuba received identity cards issued by the U.S. Justice Department; like all resident aliens, they had to notify the attorney general if they changed their address and, every January, whether they moved or not, they had to confirm their status. Ineligible for government assistance, they received social services, medical examinations, and surplus food through the federally funded Freedom Tower Refugee Center. But most aid to the Miami exiles came from the Catholic Church. The Catholic Hispanic Center in the Gesú Church in downtown Miami offered food, child care, English lessons, and job counseling. Among the other volunteer relief agencies that came to the exiles' rescue were the

Freedom Flight exiles arriving in Miami, 1966. Photo: University of Miami Special Collections

Welcoming Freedom Flight arrivals to Miami, 1966. Photo: University of Miami Special Collections

Protestant Latin American Emergency Committee and the New York–based Hebrew Immigrant Aid Society.[6]

Many of these first-wave Cubans had visited the United States before or had done business with U.S. firms—they understood how things worked. Yet even those most tuned in to the system took it for granted that Washington would not permit Castro to stay in power. Almost none of the first exiles came to the United States intending to remain.

Cuban Jewish volunteers, 1966, at the kiosk that supplied free snacks and soft drinks to Cuban refugees arriving in Miami on the Freedom Flights. Some twelve thousand Jews left Cuba after Castro's takeover. In Miami, Cuban Jews founded the Cuban-Hebrew Congregation (Temple Beth Shmuel) and the Sephardic Congregation of Florida (Temple Moses or Torat Moshe). PHOTO: BERNARDO BENES FAMILY

César Pérez Abreu being processed for U.S. citizenship, 1967. Many exiles did not file for citizenship. One man decades later explained he had never applied because the processing fee was twenty dollars higher than the price of a "green card." PHOTO: HISTORICAL MUSEUM OF SOUTHERN FLORIDA

The Cubans who arrived in Miami beginning in 1962 came from a broader social and economic spectrum. Many were professionals and businessmen whose homes and businesses had been seized in the name of the revolution; others were middle-class people who found that they could not

Victoria Cruz clips the fingernails of her father, 107-year-old Pierre Bidart, just arrived in Hialeah from Cuba, 1971. PHOTO: HISTORICAL MUSEUM OF SOUTHERN FLORIDA

Disembarking from an airplane from Havana, 1971. PHOTO: HISTORICAL MUSEUM OF SOUTHERN FLORIDA

live in Cuba under Castro. Both groups faced difficulties aggravated by political events on both sides of the Straits of Florida. President Eisenhower had refused to meet with Castro when he came to the United Nations in April 1959, and when the U.S. State Department demanded compensation

Greeting family members disembarking from a Pan Am plane, 1972. PHOTO: HISTORICAL MUSEUM OF SOUTHERN FLORIDA

Guillermo Francisco Herrera, eighty-six, just after arriving from Cuba, 1973. Many exiles over forty-five, able to find only the most menial of jobs, suffered from a condition Miami Cubans, always optimistic, called "melancholy"—actually, depression. PHOTO: HISTORICAL MUSEUM OF SOUTHERN FLORIDA

Cubans picketing the American Legion convention where Secretary of State Henry Kissinger was speaking, 1974. Kissinger was not considered sufficiently anti-Communist, perhaps because he had started to negotiate with the North Vietnamese. PHOTO: HISTORICAL MUSEUM OF SOUTHERN FLORIDA

Cuban lawyers protesting the English-language bar exam at Dade County Auditorium, 1975. PHOTO: HISTORICAL MUSEUM OF SOUTHERN FLORIDA

for nationalized U.S. businesses in Cuba, Castro stepped up his anti-American tirades. (Secretly, he also began to acquire arms from the Soviet Union.)[7] When Castro seized American oil refineries in Cuba, Eisenhower retaliated by reducing the U.S. quota for Cuban sugar, a serious blow to the island's economy.

In January 1961, more than sixty anti-Castro exile groups in Miami met to discuss combining forces. The first such group, the Anti-Castro Liberation Alliance, had organized only months after the first exiles arrived in 1959. Among its leaders were two former officers from Castro's forces, Pedro Díaz Lanz and Nino Díaz. As a result of the January meeting, the Revolutionary Movement of the People and the Democratic Front—two of the largest organizations—merged to form the National Revolutionary Council. Heading it up was José Miró Cardona, once Castro's prime minister. Quietly, most militant exile groups began to train volunteers for an invasion of Cuba. Word leaked out soon enough, and exiles from all walks of life volunteered. Businessmen donated large sums of money. Physicians joined the volunteer ranks. A contingent of Hungarian freedom fighters enlisted.[8]

Protesters demanding the right to be use Spanish in dealing with the government, 1976. Cubans' Spanish and their cultural links to the rest of Latin America greatly facilitated Miami's development as a major center for commerce and made the city the trade gateway to Latin America. PHOTO: HISTORICAL MUSEUM OF SOUTHERN FLORIDA

Despondent in exile, ex-President Carlos Prío Socarrás committed suicide in 1977. The photograph shows his grave marker at Woodland Park Cemetery.

PHOTO: ROBERT M. LEVINE

Miami's exile groups were not alone in preparing to invade the island. When John F. Kennedy became president in January 1961, he was advised that the CIA was helping to train troops in Guatemala and elsewhere to attack Cuba. Kennedy approved a reorganized plan that led to the creation of Brigade 2506, an invasion force of 1,297 volunteer soldiers advised by U.S. military personnel. The combat brigade took its name from the membership number of Carlos "Carlay" Rodríguez Santana, who was killed during a training accident. In mid-April, Brigade 2506 went ashore at the Bay of Pigs

Rally at Bicentennial Park against President Jimmy Carter's Cuban policy, considered weak and appeasing, 1977. PHOTO: HISTORICAL MUSEUM OF SOUTHERN FLORIDA

Calle Ocho (Southwest 8th Street) rally by Alpha 66, the political-military organization advocating armed struggle to combat the Castro regime, 1977. PHOTO: HISTORICAL MUSEUM OF SOUTHERN FLORIDA

and Girón beach, where they found 20,000 Cuban troops waiting for them. Tipped off by a feigned invasion two days before, Castro had not only marshaled his troops but rounded up 100,000 Cuban citizens deemed possible supporters of the invasion. Some of the captured brigadists were packed into a sealed refrigeration truck and transported more than a hundred miles to prison; nine died of suffocation. The rest remained in Cuban prisons for two years before negotiations won their release in December 1962.

The Cuban volunteers who had trained in Guatemala and been shipped to Nicaragua were astounded when their U.S. military trainers told them they had been ordered to stay out of the Bay of Pigs invasion because "things are going to be bad," according to one bitter veteran. U.S. Air Force B-26 bombers that Kennedy had promised would provide air cover never took off. U.S. Navy destroyers, submarines, and other warships expected to support the invasion sat at anchor in the Gulf of Florida. Castro's troops defeated Brigade 2506 in three days. Of the brigade's 1,297 men, 80 died in the fighting, 37 drowned, and the rest were sentenced to thirty years in prison. Seven were executed as Batista-era war criminals. More than a year

Protesters holding the Cuban flag, 1977. Some demonstrators sang an anti-Castro patriotic song whose words refer to the dictator as "the traitor who used to be our brother." PHOTO: HISTORICAL MUSEUM OF SOUTHERN FLORIDA

Continental National Bank vice president Bernardo Benes hands a letter and family photos to Combinado del Este Prison inmate Yamil Kourí, Havana, 1978. During the Carter administration, Benes's negotiations with Fidel Castro led to the release of 3,600 Cuban political prisoners and permission for exiles to visit relatives in Cuba. Photo: Historical Museum of Southern Florida

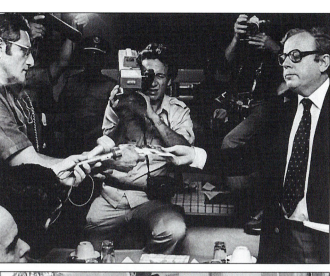

Members of Congreso de los Municipios demonstrating against Bernardo Benes across from the Continental National Bank of Miami, 1978. Many exile organizations opposed Benes's—or any—negotiations with Castro. But the negotiations would in the end trigger the massive Mariel boat lift two years later. Photo: Historical Museum of Southern Florida

Rally at Hialeah City Hall, 1978. U.S. negotiator Bernardo Benes remained under FBI protection for many years. Under the Reagan and Bush administrations, he negotiated with Cuba on such sensitive matters as communications between the CIA and Cuban DGI directors. Photo: Historical Museum of Southern Florida

later, on December 29, 1962, President Kennedy appeared at Florida's Orange Bowl to welcome home 1,113 Bay of Pigs prisoners, who had been exchanged for $53 million in food and medicine.[9]

Although the Bay of Pigs disaster had further strained diplomatic relations between Cuba and the United States, commercial flights continued to carry exiles off the island. After immigration quotas had been reached, the U.S. Embassy waived visas for Cubans, recognizing them as parolees—exiles from a Communist government. On the island, Castro's police imprisoned more than forty thousand people and executed as many as ten thousand more. On April 16, 1961, Castro proclaimed himself a Marxist-

Jorge Mas Canosa, chairman of the Cuban American National Foundation, and Juanita Castro (Fidel's sister) (on either side of the U.S. flag), May 1984. Mas Canosa created the CANF and converted it into the exiles' most powerful anti-Castro political and lobbying group. The CANF promoted programs such as Exodus to bring to the United States refugees from third countries and lobbied hard for passage of the Helms-Burton Act, which tightened the economic embargo. PHOTO: HISTORICAL MUSEUM OF SOUTHERN FLORIDA

Jorge Mas Canosa poster at his tomb at Miami's Woodlawn Park Cemetery. After his death in 1997, the Cuban American National Foundation lost some of its influence on U.S. policy toward Cuba. PHOTO: ROBERT M. LEVINE

Leninist and announced that Cuba was now a socialist country. The Bay of Pigs invasion began at sunrise the following day.

The Soviet Union, immediately after the Bay of Pigs failure, placed medium-range missiles in Cuba pointed at the United States. In October 1962, President Kennedy ordered a naval blockade of the island, thereby moving the world perilously close to nuclear war. According to KGB and CIA files made available later, Fidel Castro prodded Soviet minister Nikita Khruschev to launch the first strike. But the Soviets responded to Kennedy's action by removing most of the missiles, and war was averted. The United States did not know, however, that as many as forty nuclear missiles were secretly kept in Cuba.[10]

With the Cuban missile crisis, Castro halted all direct flights to Miami. By a count that November, as many as 195,000 Cubans had already entered the United States: 62,000 in 1960, 67,000 in 1961, and 66,000 in 1962. For almost three years, Cubans could not legally travel to the United States from the island. Refugees could reach the United States only clandestinely or via another country. Spain, Venezuela, and Mexico became popular conduits.

Fico Rojas and other Brigade 2506 veterans, April 17, 1985, at a ceremony at the Miami monument that commemorates the Bay of Pigs invasion. PHOTO: HISTORICAL MUSEUM OF SOUTHERN FLORIDA

Ronald Reagan supporter, 1986. Many new Cuban American citizens registered as Republicans, helping end the historic Democratic Party hold on Greater Miami. Florida politicians such as Claude Pepper, Bob Graham, and Dante Fascell offered support to Cuban exile causes while maintaining their New Deal–style outlook. Reagan was immensely popular among the exiles, and after his presidency South Florida became a Republican stronghold.

PHOTO: JUAN CARLOS ESPINOSA

The U.S. government, however, labeled these exiles aliens and therefore subject to immigration restrictions.

The missile crisis only added to the frustrations of exiles in South Florida, still confused by the U.S. government's apparent inability or unwillingness to remove Castro from power. Many new arrivals in the 1960s organized to keep their struggle against him alive. A few organizations continued to fight for his overthrow—veterans of the Bay of Pigs invasion, and Alpha 66 and Omega 7. In 1964, the Bacardi Rum Corporation, headed by Pepín Bosch, helped pay for a referendum in Miami to select representatives to a broad-based exile front, named the Representación Cubana del Exilio

Miami Mayor Xavier Suárez, spring 1987, speaks to anti-Communist demonstrators with his aide Lincoln Díaz-Balart at his side. In 1998, a few weeks into his second elected term, Suárez would be removed from office for having committed voter fraud. PHOTO: JUAN CARLOS ESPINOSA

Woman wrapped in a Cuban flag, 1987, holds up a photo of her brother, executed by the Castro regime. PHOTO: JUAN CARLOS ESPINOSA

Demonstrators storm the Torch of Friendship in downtown Miami, 1987, after anti-Contra demonstrators were evacuated by bus. Cuban exiles supported Nicaraguan anti-Sandinista guerrillas, the Contras, viewing the Sandinistas as Castro puppets and Communists. PHOTO: JUAN CARLOS ESPINOSA

(RECE). One of its leaders, Jorge Mas Canosa, would ultimately achieve national influence as head of the Cuban American National Foundation (CANF). But the RECE failed to represent all Cuban exiles, and its influence waned.[11]

In September 1965, to create a new disturbance, Castro reopened the gates for relatives of exiles, whom Cuban officials permitted to leave from the port of Camarioca in Matanzas province. About 2,866 seized the opportunity.[12] In November, officials of the Lyndon Johnson administration and the Cuban government, with the assistance of the Swiss embassy in Havana, signed a "memorandum of understanding." The result was two daily flights from Varadero airport east of Havana to Miami, which came to be known popularly as the Bridge to Freedom, or the Freedom Flights.

In every month from December 1, 1965, to April 6, 1973, between 3,000 and 4,000 exiles fled Cuba for Miami—297,318 persons in seven years. Most were urban whites, with the exception of as many as 8,000 Cubans of Chinese origin. Many of the new arrivals were elderly or infirm relatives of Cubans already in Miami. Most of the rest came from lower middle- and working-class backgrounds, although the educational levels of even these exiles were higher than the average for the Cuban population as a whole. Only a small handful came from provinces other than Havana and Las Villas. None of these newcomers were men of military age, who were still barred from emigrating, as were people with skills of use to the Castro government, who had to remain at least until replacements were found and trained. Sometimes this meant two or three years of forced manual agricultural labor before visas were granted.[13]

U.S. authorities encouraged these newly arriving Cubans to resettle somewhere other than Miami, for fear that the city's outspoken and burgeoning Cuban population might disrupt the metropolis. Jobs in Miami

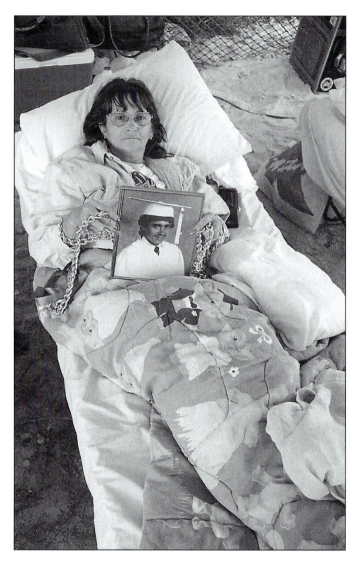

Marta Berros during the first days of the Krome Avenue hunger strike, April 1999. Berros holds a photograph of her son. She was one of six strike participants, all with children among the more than two thousand Cuban prisoners convicted of felonies who have served their terms yet still face an indefinite period of incarceration. The strike lasted a month and a half. Despite being considered a habitual offender, Berros's son was one of those the INS released as a result of the strike, several of whom have since committed new offenses and are back in jail. PHOTO: ROBERT M. LEVINE

were still scarce, especially for anyone with poor English skills. Thousands of Cubans, then, resettled in New Jersey, New York, Chicago, and Boston. A few months after the first Freedom Flights, 2,500 cities and towns across the United States had become home to Cubans. Some of these exiles returned during the 1980s and 1990s to the Miami area, as opportunities widened or as older exiles chose to live with family members there. But most stayed in their new homes.

After 1971, the number of arrivals slowed, and in May 1973, angry at the U.S. embargo on trade with Cuba, Castro unilaterally ended the airlift.

Five years later, talks in Havana between Castro and a group of Miami exiles headed by banker Bernardo Benes led to an agreement to release and transfer 3,600 political prisoners from Cuba to Miami. Exiles would also be allowed to fly back to Cuba to see relatives, a condition of the agreement that abruptly and permanently changed the way on-island Cubans viewed the exiles. They had not seen the emigrants for twenty years. Assured by their government that the Cubans in Miami lived in poverty, they were amazed to see their visiting relatives robust and affluent.

The "people's government" had been lying to them. "The *gusanos* [worms] have become butterflies," they marveled.

Marielitos and Rafters

BETWEEN MAY AND SEPTEMBER 1980, more emigrants left Cuba than in any other single year—124,769 in five months—up from 3,000 in 1979. Fidel Castro, El Comandante, had announced an airlift to Panama and Costa Rica and opened the port at Mariel—more than fifteen thousand Miamians registered at Opa-Locka Airport to fill out forms that would allow them to bring relatives over from the island. When islanders were notified that their names were on the list to go to the United States, many who had never dreamed they would be allowed to emigrate headed immediately for the docks. Unlike the earlier groups of immigrants to South Florida, the Marielitos, as this group came to be called, were roughly one-third nonwhite, and many came from either the countryside or urban lower-class backgrounds.

Pent-up frustration in Cuba, exacerbated by domestic economic problems and the "baby boom" of the 1970s, had reached the boiling point on April 11, when a Cuban bus driver crashed his vehicle through the gates of Havana's Peruvian Embassy and asked for political asylum. Within hours, 10,000 more Cubans had entered the embassy grounds, also demanding asylum. The international press covered the incident, which ignited waves of protest by Cubans in Miami against Castro's government.

The Comandante's decision to open the floodgates was less a humanitarian than a calculated act. On top of the island's economic problems, President Jimmy Carter had spoken out in support of the Cuban asylum seekers. Now Castro not only let ordinary men and women leave from Mariel, but emptied the inmates of Cuban jails and mental hospitals onto the vessels there. In some cases, the released patients and prisoners sailed to the United States under restraints.

Meanwhile, hundreds of boats set out from South Florida ports to rescue relatives and other escapees. Some of these boats, chartered by exiles, were forced by Cuban officials to take strangers aboard for the trip back across the Florida Straits. Journalists named the boat lift the Freedom Flotilla.

In his 1980 May Day speech, Castro reviled the Marielitos as "the scum of the country—antisocials, homosexuals, drug addicts, and gamblers, who are welcome to leave Cuba if any country will have them." Researchers at Havana's Center for the Study of the Americas issued figures claiming that 40 percent of the Marielitos were robbers, 18 percent were at

Rally in downtown Miami against the conditions at Havana's Peruvian Embassy, April 11, 1980, where 10,000 Cubans seeking asylum had taken refuge. Photo: University of Miami Special Collections

risk for committing crimes, 10 percent were sexual deviants, and others had been imprisoned for acts ranging from drug selling to crimes against the state.

In all, 125,000 Cubans came to the United States in the Mariel boat lift.[1] Each day, thousands waited at Key West for buses to take them north. At a dozen Dade County centers that ranged from Tamiami Park to two former Nike missile bases, more thousands passed through a seven-stage screening process to see who would be released to join relatives and who would be

Mariel boat lift, Key West, 1980. PHOTO: HISTORICAL MUSEUM OF SOUTHERN FLORIDA

Mariel detainees are moved by bus from Key West to Krome Detention Center for processing, 1980. PHOTO: DIANA G. KIRBY

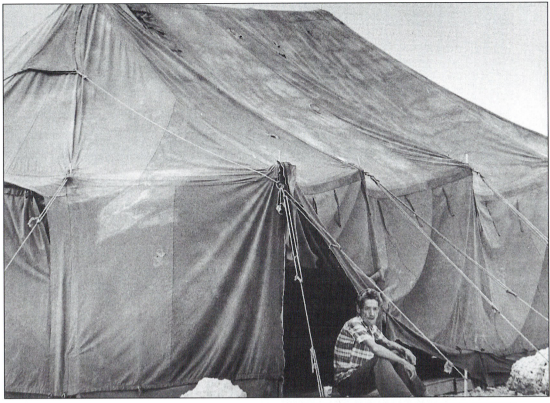

A Mariel refugee waits to be claimed by relatives or placed by immigration authorities, July 22, 1980. Most of the Mariel arrivals, in time, adjusted well and blended into the South Florida population. PHOTO: HISTORICAL MUSEUM OF SOUTHERN FLORIDA

Alberto Godals, a Mariel refugee, works at sweeping and cleaning the area outside the Orange Bowl Stadium, 1980. PHOTO: HISTORICAL MUSEUM OF SOUTHERN FLORIDA

Sunny Haven, an apartment provided for Mariel refugees, 1980. Most of the Mariel arrivals could afford to live only in tenements or other substandard housing. Much of South Florida's Cuban community was quick to respond to the needs of the Marielitos. Later, many were put off by the new arrivals' longtime experience with communism, and often by their dark skin and history of mental illness or criminality. PHOTO: HISTORICAL MUSEUM OF SOUTHERN FLORIDA

detained. Fights broke out when some claimed that Castro spies were among them.[2] In Miami, members of the Cuban Patriotic Junta gave $40 in cash to each new arrival. Washington declared the refugees immediately eligible for food stamps and earmarked $10 million for relief. Miamians donated forty tons of clothing within a few days.

But the Marielitos found it difficult to shake the misfit label, and many faced discrimination. A Cuban-born social worker, the head of a City of Miami agency, was quoted three years after their arrival as saying that one-third of the Marielitos were "trash." A highly placed Dade County school official, also Cuban American, complained that the Mariel children "[came

Modesto Mena and his wife, Marlenis Mena, 1980. The couple carries towels as they check into a downtown Miami hotel, their temporary residence after arriving from Mariel. PHOTO: HISTORICAL MUSEUM OF SOUTHERN FLORIDA

Elvira Fumero searches for relatives in the crowd at Miami International Airport, 1985. Many Cubans who had been waiting for visas in third countries were admitted to the United States in the mid-1980s.
PHOTO: HISTORICAL MUSEUM OF SOUTHERN FLORIDA

with] no concept of private property, nor that of authority as something to be respected out of admiration rather than fear."[3] By contrast, the Cuban-born assistant city manager argued that the "bad apples," as he called them, comprised less than 2.5 percent of the total.[4] Caught between two powerful political forces—Castro's government and the exile community—the "Mariel Cubans," as an exile psychologist observed, "carried the shame we all felt in having Castro outsmart us."[5] When crime in South Florida went up, fear of the Marielitos grew. Suspicion further soured public acceptance of the recent arrivals, even among Cuban Americans who had themselves been newcomers twenty years earlier.

Castro's unexpected resilience continued to frustrate Miami's exile

New arrival eight-year-old Leisy Orozco Rosas in her mother's lap, 1985. By the mid-1980s, many Cubans were listening to Radio Martí, whose broadcasts spurred their desire to leave the island at any cost. Photo: Historical Museum of Southern Florida

Former political prisoner Elia O'Farrill and her family, 1988, are greeted by friends at Miami International Airport after being released from Cuba. Photo: Historical Museum of Southern Florida

Rafters in the Florida Straits, 1994. Thousands of Cubans set off for the States in small vessels, poorly crafted rafts, and even inner tubes. After August 1984, the U.S. government refused to accept further arrivals. Rafters were intercepted in the straits and sent to camps at the U.S. Navy base in Guantanamo, where many stayed for more than a year in makeshift facilities, treated more like prisoners than refugees. PHOTO: UNIVERSITY OF MIAMI SPECIAL COLLECTIONS

Raysa Santana's son with her picture, 1995. To save the fresh water for the children aboard her raft, Santana died from drinking sea water during the voyage. PHOTO: DEMETRIO PEREZ JR. FAMILY

community, and most of the city's Cuban American interest groups remained staunchly anti-Communist. Exiles who had once supported the Democrats now moved toward the right—more than 90 percent voted for Ronald Reagan in 1980.

By 1983, three years after the Freedom Flotilla, Cubans in Miami represented 42 percent of the population, compared to 2 percent in 1959, and 14 percent in 1964. From the outset, arriving refugees had organized Cuban municipalities in exile, and 114 municipal exile groups now met in the city. Those representing Havana and Santiago de Cuba each attracted more than

Drawing by a recently arrived child, José R. Cardona, 1980s. Photo: University of Miami Special Collections

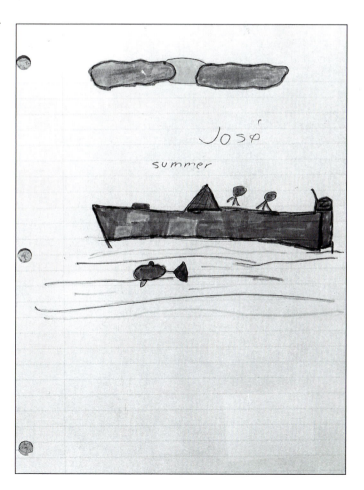

Inmates of the camp for rafters in Panama, November 1994. Some eight thousand rafters were transferred from Guantanamo to better conditions in Panama for five months. Frustration there led to a riot during which military vehicles and a camp were burned and some people were shot. PHOTO: LIDIA GONZÁLEZ-PRADA

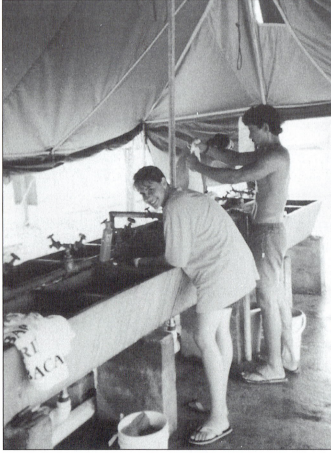

Rafters in Guantanamo camp, 1995. Many rafters spent almost a year and a half in this camp, where they reported that U.S. Marines treated them harshly. The camp's deplorable conditions eventually were alleviated by donations from Miami's Cuban community, although the language barrier remained. PHOTO: LIDIA GONZÁLEZ-PRADA

Teenage rafters from Guantanamo in Miami, late 1995. After months of detention, some exiles returned to Cuba; others were excluded by the Immigration and Naturalization Service. But most of the rafters settled into new lives in Miami.

PHOTO: UNIVERSITY OF MIAMI SPECIAL COLLECTIONS

Sisters arrive in Miami after long months in Guantanamo camp, late 1995.

PHOTO: UNIVERSITY OF MIAMI SPECIAL COLLECTIONS

Psychologist Lidia González-Prada, 1999. Now a social worker for Miami-Dade County, González-Prada displays her plastic handcuffs from Panama and Guantanamo and a compass given her by a soldier. She left Cuba with her daughter on August 24, 1994, when both Havana and Washington were permitting the boat lift, but remained in the camps until December 12, 1995. Her son had landed safely in Key West days before Clinton's order to turn back the rafters.

PHOTO: ROBERT M. LEVINE

a thousand members. Smaller groups gathered once or twice a year. High on their priorities list were promoting the values of their cultural heritage, keeping up the pressure against accommodation with Castro, and helping needy members. Some political groups who at first came together to overthrow Castro now sought to influence local, state, and national politics in the United States. Miami, to one commentator, had become "the border town between Cuba and the United States."[6]

The city's twenty-five-year-old Cuban American community had prospered, with an estimated total income of $6 billion. Its leaders encouraged the Reagan administration to create Radio Marti, a U.S. radio station that began broadcasting news, sports, music, and political programming to Cuba.

In retaliation, Havana suspended the visits of U.S. Cubans to relatives on the island, which had been permitted since the early 1980s; they were reestablished on a limited basis a year later. In 1987, Cuba agreed to accept the return of 2,000 jailed "undesirables" from the Mariel boat lift. Washington agreed to increase its quota to 20,000 Cuban immigrants a year, but for many bureaucratic reasons, the numbers reached that level only much later.[7]

The Castro regime's execution in 1989 of Angolan war hero General Arnaldo Ochoa and other military and intelligence officers sparked the first anti-government graffiti campaign on the island since Cuba had been under communist rule.

In the early 1990s, the implosion of the former Soviet Union and its East European satellites isolated Cuba. When a *Miami Herald* editorial in 1992 opposed the Torricelli bill, which would have toughened the U.S. embargo against the country, the Cuban American National Foundation placed ads in English and Spanish on the backs of sixty Miami buses reading "I Don't Believe the *Miami Herald*." Newspaper vending boxes were vandalized, and the *Herald*'s publishers received death threats.[8] Congress passed the bill, the embargo was tightened, and Miami Cubans who opposed it or favored more relaxed relations with Castro were called Communists and stooges of Castro. El Comandante blamed Washington for the growing pressure by Cuban citizens to leave the island, pointing to the embargo and the State Department's decision to issue fewer visas. The more likely cause was Cuba's economic failures.

Now more and more Cubans tried to escape the island by sea, trusting their lives to decaying boats and crude rafts, some made of inner tubes. In 1993, the apex of the new wave of migration, 3,600 arrived as *balseros*, or "rafters." Hundreds had been saved by unpaid volunteer pilots flying for

Hermanos al Rescate (Brothers to the Rescue), whose search-and-rescue flights scoured the Florida Straits for rafters. The pilots dropped life vests, food, and water before contacting the Coast Guard to pick up the boat people and take them to shore.[9]

Rioting erupted in Havana's Malecón in early August 1994, as twenty to thirty thousand protesters smashed windows and chanted anti-regime slogans. On August 12, Castro abruptly allowed boats to leave the island from any port. The U.S. Coast Guard picked up more than 36,000 *balseros* over the next five weeks.[10]

After letting the newest wave of exiles into the country, the United States at this point refused to countenance another Mariel. The remaining refugees—40,000—were forced by the Coast Guard to take "safe haven" at the U.S. naval base at Guantanamo, Cuba. U.S. and Cuban officials agreed to negotiate. During the next several months, the departure of boats from Cuba virtually stopped; in turn, Washington issued humanitarian visas for some of the Guantanamo detainees, but most remained, under very poor conditions, at the base. Some agreed to go to Panama; after months of waiting, the Cubans who remained interned at a base there rioted and burned down part of the facility. They were then flown back to Guantanamo, where they received better treatment than that during their earlier internment.

Although a trickle of Cubans managed to enter the United States in the mid-1990s through humanitarian sponsors, most of the "rafters" had spent more than a year in detention by the time they were allowed into the country.

It took a tragedy to turn the United States decisively against Castro. On February 24, 1996, two Cuban fighter planes shot down two tiny Brothers to the Rescue planes in international air space. Four of the volunteer fliers died. Soon afterward, President Bill Clinton signed the Cuban Liberty and Solidarity Act (the Helms-Burton Act), directing the U.S. government to

Members of the Alvarez family in Cuba, before the Mariel boat lift, 1979. The family lived in Guanabacoa, a quiet district of Greater Havana. Ramiro Alvarez trucked goods from the port, carried students to the countryside, where they had been assigned to cut cane, and transported bananas and other foods unavailable in Havana from the country to the city, hidden under a tarp.

<small>Photo: Mariela Alvarez</small>

Miriela and Mariela Alvarez with their father and grandfather, first snow, 1982. The Alvarez family, who joined the boat lift with plans to live in Florida, were flown to a military base at Fort Indiantown Gap, Pennsylvania, then released after thirty days to a relative in New York City. There, the girls' father, Ramiro, worked full-time in a hardware store and part-time at three porter's jobs. Their grandfather had waited two years for a visa for this visit; U.S. officials had suspected him of really wanting to become a permanent resident.

<small>Photo: Mariela Alvarez</small>

Mariela Alvarez's first U.S. birthday party, New York City, 1980. Everyone at the party is an Alvarez relation. Five years later, the family moved to Miami, where Ramiro Alvarez bought a new truck.

<small>Photo: Mariela Alvarez</small>

impose sanctions on foreign companies trading with Cuba and using properties Castro had seized. At the same time, annual Cuban American remittances to relatives in Cuba had reached hundreds of millions of dollars. Cuba's economy, ironically, relied as much on the exile community to provide hard dollars as on Canadian and European tourists to the island.

In 1999, Castro marked his fortieth anniversary in power with a speech in which he mocked those refugees in the initial wave who had expected to stay only temporarily in South Florida—that is, virtually all of them.

Some Cuban exiles still struggle with the regulations of the U.S. Immigration and Naturalization Service (INS). The Anti-Terrorism and Effective Death Penalty Act of 1996, which mandates deportation for felons, keeps as many as 2,150 in jails. They are scheduled for deportation once Castro falls, even though they have served their prison terms.

In April 1999, five parents (four mothers and one father) of jailed sons joined in a hunger strike at the entrance to Miami's Krome Avenue Detention Center, pleading for mercy for their children, who were among these prisoners.

After several weeks, some of the strikers, who had consumed only Gatorade and were weakened by the heat, collapsed and had to be taken to the hospital. But on the forty-seventh day, the INS commissioners agreed to transfer four of the strikers' sons to Krome and to review their cases under the supervision of the Archdiocese of Miami.

Neither tighter U.S. immigration laws nor the Castro government have managed to stem the flow of Cuban refugees entirely. Frequently now they are smuggled in on boats, for the most part journeying from the Bahamas. Cubans already in South Florida have reacted to the rafters with mixed emotions. Sympathy from some has been balanced by disdain from others, who have maintained their distance.[11]

On March 31, 1999, five Cubans aboard a fifteen-foot raft made of wood and inner tubes were detained by the Coast Guard off the Florida Straits near the Tortugas. A cruise ship picked up another six men on an inflatable raft twenty-five miles off Marathon Key.[12]

On Thanksgiving Day 1999, a five-year-old boy, Elián González, was found floating in an inner tube, surrounded by dolphins, by two fishermen off the coast of Florida. His mother, stepfather, and seven others accompanying him had drowned en route from Cuba. When the boy was taken in by relatives in Miami, with the support and sympathy of the exile community, Fidel Castro orchestrated massive demonstrations of hundreds of thousands of Cubans, demanding that Elián, just turned six, be returned to his father on the island.

The INS, Attorney General (and Miamian) Janet Reno, and President Bill Clinton said Elián should be sent back to his father. Elián's case engulfed Miami as the year 2000 opened. The reaction in Miami was spontaneous and angry. Many exiles identified deeply with the mother's desperate effort to bring her son to the United States. Cuban American organizations engineered public protests, including blocking traffic, and simultaneously worked with state and national politicians to prevent any return by making the boy a U.S. citizen. The child custody impasse symbolized the anguish of decades of family divisions.

The Flavors of Transition

WHEN THEY ARRIVED IN MIAMI, most of the early Cuban exiles found housing in Riverside, a fading-class neighborhood through which Southwest 8th Street stretched some twenty or so blocks west from the Miami River separating it from downtown. Others were placed in apartments in Miami Beach, or in transient hotels dotted throughout the city. But so many moved into Riverside that newspapers dubbed it "Little Havana," a name that stuck.

Few of the early exiles spoke English well. They were used to living and

Miami skyline from the McArthur Causeway, 1940. PHOTO: ROMER COLLECTION, MIAMI-DADE PUBLIC LIBRARY

A view of the Miami skyline from the McArthur Causeway, 1999. PHOTO: MOISÉS Asís

doing business in enclosed communities—this is how it had been in Cuba, where decisions typically were made after consultations with friends and relatives, "and only as a last resort did they venture outside the closely knit circle of acquaintances they had known and trusted all their lives."[1] Since nearly all the professionals and entrepreneurs left Cuba about the same time, once in Miami they quickly rebuilt many of the old informal networks.

Those who had been wealthy in Cuba became distraught over the condition of even the better temporary accommodations in Little Havana. For others who had not been well off on the island, their new homes were an improvement.

By the end of the 1960s, whole Miami neighborhoods or parts of neighborhoods were largely Cuban. Cuban exile organizations instituted

Little Havana, U.S.A., 1999. Corner of Southwest 8th Street and Twenty-sixth Avenue. Republic National, the first bank owned by Cuban Americans, was sold in mid-1999 to Union Planters' Bank. On the ground floor is Chantres Cleaners, a clone of a business by the same name in Havana. PHOTO: ROBERT M. LEVINE

charitable programs; at least one television station, the local NBC affiliate, hired a Cuban American broadcaster to deliver, in English, news of interest to the Cuban community. The disorientation and hopelessness of the initial arrivals had given way to relative security and comfort.

Most Cubans chose to start their own businesses rather than seek their fortunes in the "Anglo" business community. Miami, a tourist city in the

Drinking Cuban coffee, 1982. Photo: Mariela Alvarez

Top: A "coffee window," Little Havana, 1999. Such windows preserve a Cuban tradition for customers who enjoy sipping a cup of espresso or a *cortadito* (espresso with milk) without entering a restaurant or cafeteria. Photo: Robert M. Levine

Right: Luis Fernández sips Cuban coffee at Cafetería El Fénix on Coral Way, 1987. Photo: Historical Museum of Southern Florida

Slaughtered pig hangs in a backyard,
1963. *Lechón* (roast pork) remains a
popular food at Cuban family festivities.
PHOTO: HISTORICAL MUSEUM OF SOUTHERN
FLORIDA

doldrums, offered ample opportunities. The recession of the early 1970s
created opportunities for Cuban exile businesses—their larger Anglo rivals
reacted to the slow economy in traditional ways by downsizing, while the
more scrappy Cuban enterprises filled in the vacuum. In 1967, Cuban-
owned businesses numbered 919. By 1978, their number had jumped to ten
times as many. Little Havana sprouted not only repair shops and other small
businesses but offices of accountants, physicians, and dentists who catered
to their fellow Cubans. Generously scattered throughout were the dozens of
Cuban restaurants and coffee counters and *almacenes* (grocery stores) that
gave Little Havana the distinctive flavor it retains today.[2]

Badias Restaurant postcard, 1970. The back reads: "A landmark in the heart of Little Havana for Cuban sandwiches and steaks featuring more than fifty daily gourmet delights of the continental and Spanish cuisines." Photo: University of Miami Special Collections

Cook Roberto Leyes at La Carreta restaurant in Kendall, 1987, where he serves up traditional Cuban food such as these black beans. Photo: Historical Museum of Southern Florida

Latin American Cafeteria, Hialeah, 1999. Adela Herrera chats with a fellow customer. Photo: Robert M. Levine

Wajiro's restaurant on Southwest 8th Street in West Dade, 1999. "Wajiro" is a variant of the Spanish word "guajiro," a country bumpkin. Photo: Robert M. Levine

A Montes de Oca pizza restaurant,
1999. Named for the Mariel immigrant
who developed and owns the three-
restaurant chain, the pizzerias offer such
toppings as plantains, pineapple, and
picadillo (spicy ground beef) and make
"Varadero style" pizzas, a reference to
Cuba's famous Castle Nuovo pizzeria.
Other popular Cuban pizza parlors
include Rey Pizza, Castle Nuovo, and
Sorrento. Photo: Robert M. Levine

Like all new immigrants, the Cubans cherished their own culture and
history. Many Miami businesses and restaurants claim they opened their
doors not only before the Castro regime appeared but well before the city of
Miami was founded. The claim, of course, is technically true, since they
trace their founding to their originals that opened in Cuba in earlier
decades.[3]

Inside a Sedano's supermarket, 1999. This Cuban American chain, with stores throughout Greater Miami, has expanded from its original Cuban niche to offer products popular with Miamians from all over Latin America. PHOTO: ROBERT M. LEVINE

Selecting taro tubers for preparing ajiaco stew and other Cuban dishes, 1999. PHOTO: ROBERT M. LEVINE

A story widely circulated among the city's non-Cubans is that the Versailles restaurant on Calle Ocho (Southwest 8th Street) was rebuilt in Miami with the same blueprints by which it had been constructed in Havana, and that regulars were served by the same waitresses they knew from Cuba. The problem with this story is that the original Versailles was in Santiago de

Outdoor market, West Flagler and Northwest Fifty-seventh Avenue, 1999. Vendors of wares ranging from straw hats to leather belts as well as seviche (marinated fish), barbecue, and coconut milk set up in the parking lot of a popular Cuban take-out food market. PHOTO: ROBERT M. LEVINE

Buying homemade plantain chips, West Flagler and Northwest Fifty-seventh Avenue, 1999. PHOTO: ROBERT M. LEVINE

Cuba, at the opposite end of the island from Havana. But the menu resembles those of many popular Cuban restaurants of the 1950s, and the restaurant's first waitresses may well have worked for restaurants serving Cuba's middle class before the revolution.

Dozens of restaurants and cafeterias that flourished in Cuba have Miami siblings. The exiles brought with them the names—and in many cases the appearance—of La Carreta, Ayestarán Cafeteria, Da Rosina, El Patio, Café Barcelona, Río Cristal, El Baturro, Kasalta, Emperador, El Caney, La Pelota, La Rampa, La Rosa, La Bodeguita Cubana, La Terraza de Cojímar,

Miami billboard, 1999, advertises a
brand of crackers popular in Cuba.

PHOTO: ROBERT M. LEVINE

Morro Castle, Rancho Luna, Havana Vieja, Siete Mares, Coppelia, among
many others. The famous Havana original of Miami's La Zaragozana was
reopened by the Castro regime in the late 1980s.

La Esquina de Tejas, a small restaurant on a busy corner of Little
Havana and named after a busy intersection in Havana, was made famous
by a visit from President Ronald Reagan—the street where it stands was
renamed in his honor. La Carreta, now a chain of Cuban restaurants in
Miami, resembles the original one at K and 21st Streets in Vedado, Cuba.

New versions of Cuban establishments include supermarkets (Sedano's,

Ñooo! ¡Qué Barato! bargain store in
West Hialeah, 1999, the favorite store of
Cuban Americans making visits to Cuba.

PHOTO: MOISÉS ASÍS

Varadero) and bakeries (Tosca, Capri, Casa Potín, El Brazo Fuerte, La Gran
Vía, Super Cake, LaWard, Karla, Perezsosa, La Suiza, El Lido, and La Sin
Rival). Flower shops include Trías Florist, El Gladiolo, Tosca, Trianón, and
Jardín Cuba. Funeral homes include Bernardo García, Abreu González,
Caballero Woodlawn, Funeraria Cubana, Funeraria Nacional, and Rivero.

Another echo of the old life on the island comes from the famous
Cuban brands available everywhere in Miami—none of which any longer
exist in Cuba. They include Hatuey, La Tropical, Cristal, Polar (beers and
malts); Cawy, Ironbeer, Jupiña, and Materva (soft drinks); Conchita
(desserts); La Estrella and Gilda (crackers); Edmundo cooking oil and dry
wine; Pilón, Bustelo, and La Llave coffee; and Nela, La Lechera, and Batey
condensed milk. Other brands, invented in Miami, are strongly Cuban in
flavor: Batey, Siboney, and Yarima malts; La Cubanita preserves; and La
Estrella Solitaria, Cacique, and Del Campo cheeses. The Bacardi family
brought with them from Cuba their well-known name, their formulas for
making rum, and their registered trademark.

Menus of Cuban restaurants and cafeterias in Miami today might
include *café con leche* (Cuban coffee with milk); sandwiches made on
toasted, buttered Cuban bread (lighter and more airy than its French coun-
terpart) with ham, roast pork, cheese, and pickles; *fritas* (spicy thin ham-
burgers with onions); Cuban-style rice and black beans; cream cheese and
guava pastries; and tropical fruit shakes. Once considered exotic, Cuban
food today is a staple for Miamians of every background.

Fitting In

ONE EXILE HAS DESCRIBED his childhood in the United States as isolated compared to his early years in Cuba, but happy nevertheless.

Exile had brought me a special kind of freedom. At Dade Elementary, for the first and only time in our lives, my brother Pepe and I walked to school. After school, we went home and I headed for the park or the Boy's Club, where I stayed until nightfall. In Cuba no kid in my family was allowed to walk to school, much less roam the streets. In fact, most things

The first Cubans in Hialeah, Rafael and Jorgelina Díaz and their daughter, Maggie, on the lot where their home will be built, 1955. Rafael, a Korean War veteran, was earning $3,380 a year as a transmission repairman and paid $12,550 for the house, with a monthly mortgage payment of $71.50. PHOTO: RAFAEL DÍAZ FAMILY

public were off limits to us in Havana. . . . Once in the United States,
within certain limits, we were on our own and we made the most of it.
Although I sometimes felt isolated wandering the streets all by myself, I
was happy to trade solitude for latitude.[1]

Not all Cubans wanted to make that trade-off. For many years in Miami,
if one chose to, one could stay safe inside the Cuban enclave, psychologically
if not always physically. One could work for Cuban American firms where

The Díaz house at 931 West 53d Street,
Hialeah, 1960. Adding a porch cost the
family five dollars at Hialeah City Hall for
a building permit. The Díazes shopped at a
supermarket at Northwest 62d Street and
Twelfth Avenue because it carried some
Puerto Rican brands. Photo: Rafael Díaz
family

Rafael Díaz, 1999, in front of the home
in which his family has lived since 1955.
Photo: Moisés Asís

"Inter-apartment communication, Latin-style," according to the *Miami News* caption, 1980. At Westland Eden Apartments, Lilian Figueroa and daughter Lliamel talk to Orestes Monzón and Rafael Figueroa. PHOTO: HISTORICAL MUSEUM OF SOUTHERN FLORIDA

only Spanish was spoken and tune day or night to Spanish radio—WFAB, *La Fabulosa,* and WQBA, *La Cubanísima*—and Spanish television. One could listen to pre-Castro-era Cuban music and be entertained by exiled Cuban performers and eat at Cuban restaurants. The Versailles on Calle Ocho became a meeting place, along with several other restaurants, for Cuban American businessmen and politicians.[2] Miami hosted live theater in Spanish, much of it with Cuban content. Medical services—including mental health clinics—were available to those who wanted them.

A small minority of the city's Cubans have tried to erase their Cuban heritage altogether. One young man, for instance, took the middle name

Borbon, so that he could claim a link to the Spanish royal line. Some have worked on losing their accents or have affected a non-Cuban way of speaking Spanish, often Madrileño. Some Cubans are put off by some of Miami's apparent values—for example, the city's reputation for political chicanery, reported to include the casting of ballots by registered voters from their cemetery plots. Others shrug off such practices and express the hope that with maturity, the still young and fast-changing city will show more civic responsibility.

Playing dominos in Little Havana, 1967.

PHOTO: HISTORICAL MUSEUM OF SOUTHERN FLORIDA

Most Cubans exiles have held onto at least some island customs and embraced the U.S. culture as well. The speech of many young Cubans is a perfect example. At one time, many exiles spoke Cubano—called by José Llanes in 1980 "a phonological pattern imposed on the Spanish language which makes speech go twice as fast as it usually does when Mexicans or Puerto Ricans talk." But the Cubano spoken in the United States by some-

On the way to becoming U.S. citizens, Orange Bowl Stadium, July 4, 1986. PHOTO: JUAN CARLOS ESPINOSA

Mass swearing-in of new citizens, Orange Bowl Stadium, July 4, 1986. More than ten thousand exiles became U.S. citizens during this ceremony. PHOTO: JUAN CARLOS ESPINOSA

one who left Cuba fifteen or twenty years ago, according to Llanes, was a bit stale. In the last twenty years, the language has gotten mixed up with English and the Spanish of other Hispanics, and Cubano sounds even less like it used to.[3]

Young Cubans today, in many cases, speak among themselves a language that alternates phrases of Spanish and English, switching comfortably back and forth from one language to another, although they set this speech aside when others are present.

Cultural activities offered Miami's Cubans a chance both to keep their own heritage alive and to mix with their new non-Cuban neighbors. Maria Gómez Carbonell founded Cruzada Educativa Cubana in 1962, one of the first formal Cuban cultural groups in the city. Cuban bookstores, among

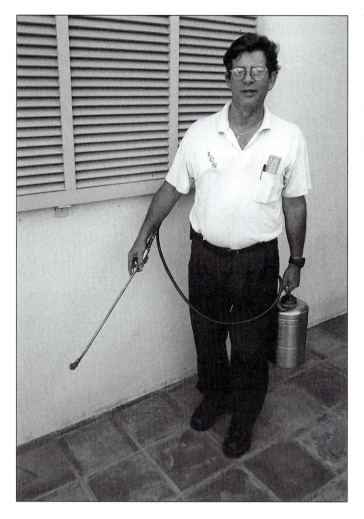

Miguel Roberto Fernández, pest-control sprayer, 1999. With a day job, a night job, and an independent cleaning service, Fernández is proud that he can offer his family a better life than would have been possible in Cuba. "I am happy," he says. PHOTO: ROBERT M. LEVINE

them Moderna Poesía and La Universal, organized literary circles. Local universities sponsored art exhibits, musical events, and seminars of interest to both Cubans and non-Cubans.[4]

Many early arrivals threw themselves almost immediately into entrepreneurship (the Cuban as well as the American way). They built their own economic enclave, with mostly Cuban customers, a trend that mushroomed in the 1970s. In Little Havana, many Cubans organized needlepoint workshops to produce piece goods and became supply contractors to established "Anglo" firms. Eventually, some of them started their own factories. Miami was not a strong labor town and few raised objections when Cuban businesses hired Cubans at wages low by industry standards but a boon to those—mostly women—who were often unable to find other work at all.

Old-style barber shop, Little Havana, 1999. Photo: Robert M. Levine

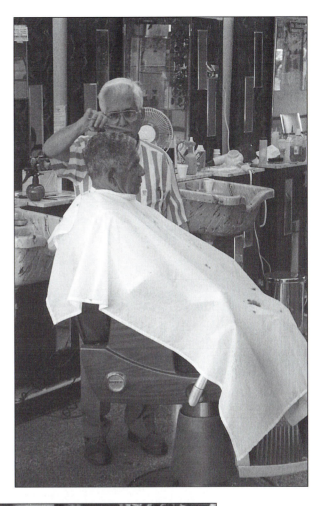

Factory, 1968. Factorias (the Spanglish version) within the enclave often employed exile workers off the books, meaning that they did not receive overtime, health insurance, or pensions. This situation survives, although many of today's workers are migrants from other Latin American countries. Photo: Historical Museum of Southern Florida

Produce truck, 1999. Many immigrants have made their living by selling vegetables, flowers, or prepared meals from trucks. Photo: Robert M. Levine

Selling merchandise out of the trunk of a car, Hialeah, 1999. Photo: Robert M. Levine

In the early days, it was not unusual for non-Cuban Miamians to resent the exiled Cubans' economic practices. Some African Americans complained that they were frequently fired when the shops and service stations at which they worked were bought by Cubans. They did not speak Spanish, and Cubans preferred to hire their fellow exiles. Anglos who resented the tendency of the early exiles to segregate themselves in Cuban Rotary Clubs, Cuban charities, and Cuban business organizations overlooked the fact that few spoke English when they arrived, and that one way to cope was to resist assimilation. Some Anglos in Miami called the Cubans "Cubanzos" and mocked their habits. In a show of solidarity, many Cuban Americans

Man (hiding behind pole) selling plastic trinkets, 1999. Hialeah is both the center of the underground (or "informal") economy and the site of the heaviest concentration of industry in Miami-Dade County. PHOTO: ROBERT M. LEVINE

"Envíos a Cuba," Hialeah, 1999. Miami is dotted with shops that ship goods to Cuba. Almost all island Cubans have relatives in the United States and often depend on them for medicines and other necessities they cannot obtain in Cuba. Many Miami Cubans suspect that the Castro government shares in the profits of some stores whose business is very lucrative. PHOTO: ROBERT M. LEVINE

El Indio Bakery, Hialeah, 1999. This bakery/cafeteria caters to the large Cuban American working class. PHOTO: ROBERT M. LEVINE

adopted the term as an endearing label for people who insisted on remaining conventional or on holding staunchly to Cuban tradition.

What began as an economic recovery limited to Miami's Cuban Americans expanded to other Hispanics, then to the entire metropolitan region, and finally to the region's export economy. By 1978, South Florida exported more than $6 billion in goods, most of them to Latin America.[5] Miami became, according to a popular saying, "the capital of Latin America." The enclave expanded, eventually reaching into banking, communications, construction, manufacturing, retail sales, automobile sales, and local politics—all sectors once dominated by Anglos.

A boat and vehicles fill the yard of a Hialeah home, 1999. Many Cubans have bought boats in hopes of someday returning to Cuba to retrieve relatives. Photo: Robert M. Levine

West Miami home, 1999. The cement cones near the driveway are common throughout South Florida, set out to discourage parking on the grass. Photo: Robert M. Levine

As Cubans began to move to outlying Miami neighborhoods, especially those housing families with higher income levels, some Anglo families relocated north of the Dade County line or to Florida's west coast, where they could live in a less "Hispanic" environment.

Race has played a subtle role within the Cuban community itself. In pre-1959 Cuba, as in the United States, blacks stood at the bottom of the economic scale, although Cuba had no segregation laws and was far less racist than the United States or Western Europe. Fulgencio Batista, who was a mulatto, was referred to without racial disparagement as "El Indio." Discrimination as practiced in Cuba was informal. Cuban hotel owners, if

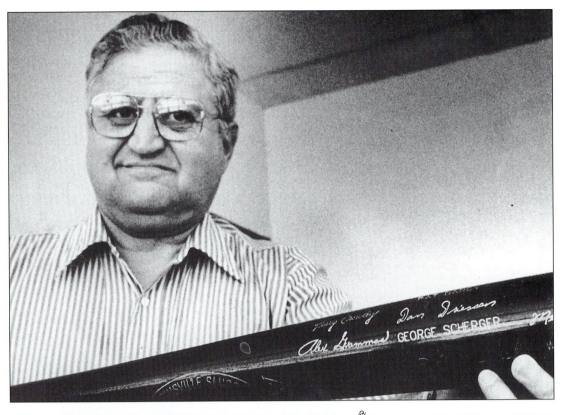

Bobby Maduro, 1976, a major figure in Cuban baseball before 1959. In Florida, Maduro ran the minor-league Miami Marlins. A stadium in South Florida has been named for him. Among the many Cuban baseball players raised in and living in Miami are José Canseco, Alex Fernández, and Jorge Fábregas. PHOTO: HISTORICAL MUSEUM OF SOUTHERN FLORIDA

Liván Hernández, 1999. Hernández defected from Cuba before the 1997 season and played with the Florida Marlins to win the World Series that year. He was traded to the San Francisco Giants in the middle of the 1999 season. On his emotional return to Miami in August 1999, he pitched seven impressive innings before being relieved. PHOTO: DENIS BANCROFT, FLORIDA MARLINS

questioned about why they banned blacks as guests, blamed their American clientele: "Americans want this."

One young woman, born in Miami to a traditional Cuban family, tells this story. "One humid day," she said, "I was having a terrible time with my hair.... I joked with my mother, who had entered my room, that maybe one of our ancestors had been African. My mother turned red and walked over to me, and she slapped me hard across the face. I learned that you do not joke about these things to your parents."[6]

One of the unstated reasons for the Cuban community's relative lack of support for post-1980 arrivals is that so many not only were working class and raised on communism, but had darker skin coloration than the exiles of the 1960s. The rafters have had a harder time adapting than earlier exiles. Having grown up in communist Cuba, they are bewildered by American life. The middle waves—men and women who arrived from the late 1960s to the early 1990s, including those who came from Mariel—have perhaps assimilated more easily, as have the children of the first exiles, who brought with them their extended families and their business and social contacts. Even living side by side, Cubans who arrived in the first wave and the rafters often remain aloof from one another. Some of the older Cuban Americans have spoken out against the new arrivals. "Their life-style and way of thinking is different," one told a reporter. "Deep down they feel we owe them something, that we've had it better."[7]

All along, one way the exiles have coped with the longevity of Castro's regime is humor. Jokes in the Cuban community—many of them political—spread like wildfire. One difference between these jokes and the ones popular among other Latin Americans is that, in Cuban jokes, Cubans always win. (Colombians, Argentines, and Mexicans, for example, are typically self-deprecating.) Jokes against Castro have circulated even on the

Cartoon: "Culture Shock" by José M. Varela. After answering recorded questions asking if he is an American citizen or a legal resident (3 and 5), the caller is asked by his wife (7), "Sweetie, have you gotten through yet?" "These Americans," he replies (8), "demand to know too much. They must be half-Communists." "Liberals," she says.

island, where telling one in public can lead to arrest and conviction for spreading "enemy propaganda."

In the United States, a popular anti-Castro joke among Cuban Americans in the 1980s also poked fun at Cuba:

Q: What is the world's biggest country?

A: Cuba, because its capital is in Havana, its money in Switzerland, its colony in Nicaragua, its cemetery in Africa, its factories in Moscow, its people in Miami, and it is governed from Hell.

Moving Up

A FORTUNATE FEW among the first Cuban exiles to arrive in Miami carried jewelry with them or had managed to ship other valuables off the island. For the other early arrivals, often heads of families who had in Cuba been business owners or professionals with comfortable lives, earning a living in Miami posed immense difficulties.

Many exiles moved into small, hot apartments in Little Havana and walked the streets looking for work. Since only menial, low-paying jobs were available to them, husbands and wives both had to find work, including women who had always been housewives. Many exiles were unable to find formal jobs because they lacked the INS's green cards; local labor unions protected their members' interests by lobbying against programs that would make it easier for the exiles to gain employment. Cuban accountants, doctors, and lawyers found themselves toiling in factories or pumping gas, driving taxis or shelving stock, often "off the books" and therefore without benefits. [1]

Architects and civil engineers learned that not only was certification difficult to obtain, but South Florida building codes prohibited the use of many of the methods and materials used in Cuba. The leading building-trade professionals, then, went not to South Florida but to Puerto Rico, where codes were less stringent (and less influenced by the construction industry).

In the mid-1960s, after Cuban builders had shown what they could do in San Juan, Bacardi sponsored the petition of several Cuban architects and engineers to work in Miami. One architectural firm, SACMAG, successfully tackled the problem of constructing highrise buildings in downtown Miami, which sits on mostly sand, and therefore contributed significantly to the city's urban growth.

A number of the early exiles eventually left Little Havana, moving north

Gilbert Arriaza decorates a cake in his first bakery, 1976. This family-owned bakery now has locations all over Miami as well as a mail-order business. Photo: Gilbert Arriaza family

The opening of a new Gilbert's Bakery, one of many successful Cuban American chain-store enterprises, at Bird Road and Red Road, 1996. Photo: Gilbert Arriaza family

Costa Nursery Farms, Inc., Homestead, 1999. The Cuban family-owned business that began in the 1960s as a small tomato farm is today a wholesale distributor of nursery plants all over the United States. Photo: Patricia García-Vélez

and west into North Dade's Hialeah. The first Cuban grocery there—Coqui's—opened during the late 1960s at Twelfth Avenue and West 49th Street. Coqui's sold beans, rice, and Cuban cuts of meat. The butcher let those who could not pay buy meat on account. The market became the hub of the Cuban community—mothers with their children shopped there every Saturday afternoon for staples for the coming week. Everyone talked ardently about their old lives in Cuba, where they had lived, and what they would do when they returned. During the 1970s, some builders actually started to construct on Biscayne Boulevard a replica of Havana's prestigious Miramar neighborhood. The project was never completed, although the

Samy (Samuel Suárez), one of the world's top hair stylists, has his own product line and his own show on Univision, the Spanish-language TV network. Samy grew up in Chicago after his parents fled Cuba in 1962. He moved to Miami on his own in 1972, where he started at a beauty salon as number seventeen—only after seventeen customers had come in was he allowed a turn. Photo courtesy of Samy

Cashiers at Navarro Discount Pharmacy, South Miami, 1999. This successful chain is owned by the same family that started the business in Cuba. Its clientele is largely Hispanic. Photo: Patricia García-Vélez

Bacardi family crypt, Woodlawn Cemetery, 1999. The family business established by Don Facundo Bacardi in Santiago de Cuba in 1862 is now worth more than a billion dollars. Bacardi Rum, which supports many Cuban American philanthropies, today owns Dewar's, B&B, Bombay Gin, and Martini & Rossi. Photo: Robert M. Levine

beautiful Priscilla and Algonquin apartments, in the Mediterranean style, remain.

After 1980, when working-class Cubans began to arrive, many settled in Hialeah, where housing cost less than in Little Havana. As they moved in, families enjoying moderate economic success renovated and added on to their first homes or moved to such middle-class suburbs as Westchester, Kendall, and Miami Springs. The more economically successful flocked to the handsome, high-density real estate developments with Spanish names in West Kendall and beyond Westchester to West Miami. The most well-to-do Cuban Americans moved out to more fashionable neighborhoods such as Coral Gables, which had been founded in the 1920s to exclude such undesirables as Jews and Latinos. There large homes were set on beautifully landscaped grounds, many on canals or facing Biscayne Bay. One young woman from a family with no relatives left in Cuba remarked in 1999: "I have never been to Hialeah and have no reason to do so."[2]

Members of Miami's Cuban community have succeeded not only economically but in every other area of life—educational, political, and cultural. Although Luis J. Botifoll was not one of the exiles forced to start from nothing, his is an early Cuban American success story. Born in Havana in 1908 to a family of Spanish immigrants, Botifoll graduated in law from the University of Havana in 1930 and from Tulane University in 1931. In Cuba, he practiced law, and from 1949 to 1955 he was the editor of *El Mundo*, a Havana newspaper. Replaced by a Batista crony, Botifoll left for Florida in August 1960. During his first three years in Miami he devoted himself full-time to exile causes. In 1968, he bought a handsome house in Coral Gables, in which he still lives. Two years later, he joined a group of Cubans who had purchased the Republic National Bank. He became a member of the board in 1970 and from 1978 to 1993 served as its chairman.

In the years since Botifoll became a force outside the Cuban commu-

Natalie Beller Lyons in front of her house, Coral Gables, 1999. Born in Havana to Romanian grandparents whose children settled in Key West, Lyons came to the United States in 1942 and in 1967 moved to Coral Gables, which reminded her of Havana, minus its hills. She became one of the first "Hispanics" (and Jews) to live in the community, established in 1925.
Photo: Robert M. Levine

Luis and Aurora Botifoll in their Coral Gables home, 1999. Luis Botifoll, ninety-two, a founder of the Cuban American National Foundation and a longtime trustee of the University of Miami, points out that his compatriots were exiles, not immigrants, a key to understanding their success: They arrived highly educated and experienced in business. Photo: Robert M. Levine

Congresswoman Ileana Ros-Lehtinen with her daughters, Amanda Michelle and Patricia Marie, 1998. Here they examine the tags at the annual Salvation Army "Adopt an Angel" event at Dadeland Mall, which provides toys for needy children at Christmas. Ros-Lehtinen, who left Cuba at the age of seven a non-English speaker, was the first Cuban American woman elected to Congress. Her family paid round-trip fares on Pan American Airways from Havana, and she still possesses the return half of her ticket. Photo: Ileana Ros-Lehtinen family

nity, other Cuban Americans have reached similar prominence. Modesto Maidique heads Florida International University, and Carlos de la Cruz chairs the University of Miami's board of trustees. Other Cuban Americans have directed the city's largest banks and corporations, headed its largest real estate development firm, and moved up in its largest law firm to managing partner.[3]

Congressman Lincoln Diaz-Balart, his wife, Cristina Diaz-Balart, and their sons, Lincoln Gabriel and Daniel, 1999. With one of the most conservative congressional voting records, the Republican legislator staunchly defends the anti-Castro embargo and has fought in Congress to enlarge the scope of laws protecting immigrants from Latin America.
Photo: Picture Works, Inc., Miami

José Enrique Souto at his family-owned Café Pilón factory, 1999. In Cuba, the Souto family had run a coffee business since the 1870s, but they started over with nothing in Miami. Eventually they purchased the Café Pilón name and built a large modern plant. Today, ten family members work for Café Pilón, as well as 125 employees. "Cubans didn't make Miami," Souto says, "but we helped." PHOTO: ROBERT M. LEVINE

MasTec Corporation truck from the construction corporation owned by the Mas Canosa family, 1999. PHOTO: ROBERT M. LEVINE

On the economic scene, by the 1970s, Cuban exiles had transformed the city. The Clínica Asociación Cubana (CAC), for example, opened in 1970 in Little Havana. Based on the popular *clínicas* operating in Cuba since the 1920s, the CAC, founded by Benjamín León and Moisés Liber, pioneered the field of community medicine in the United States. Within seven years, the CAC had expanded to two centers with more than thirty thousand members. During the 1980s the company became Florida's first HMO to offer services

Downtown Miami financial district,
1999. PHOTO: MOISÉS ASÍS

to Medicare patients. In 1994, after several mergers, it emerged as United
HealthCare Corporation, serving 20 million members. CAC still runs
twenty-five clinics in Miami.[4]

Another striking example of Cuban entrepreneurs successfully com-
peting with U.S. businesses is the Pollo Tropical chain, whose fast-food
chicken outlets can be found today throughout South Florida.

By the 1980s, the combined purchasing power of Miami's Cubans
exceeded the total purchasing power of Cubans still on the island. Miami-
Dade County in 1996 exported $24.5 billion in goods, while Cuba as a whole
in 1997 exported only $1.9 billion.[5] Today, Miami has emerged as the com-
mercial gateway to Latin America, a circumstance aided in no small mea-
sure by the fact that visitors feel comfortable speaking Spanish in Miami
and find there a sophisticated Hispanic urban culture.

Cartoon: "At the Office," by José M. Varela. This cartoon pokes fun at the reputation of some Cuban American firms for overworking their Cuban employees. The loudspeaker is announcing to office workers that they are expected to donate for the boss's birthday gift. A tiny box for complaints and suggestions stands beside a large one for tattling on fellow employees. One of the signs reads, "The boss is always correct," and a former Castro bodyguard mans the exit door, which opens only at 9 A.M. and 5 P.M.

The entrepreneurial spirit is still healthy in the late 1990s. America Vaughan, who emigrated from Cuba in the early 1960s and who married a U.S. Navy officer, started a soft-drink company, Havana Cola, in 1998. Facing the near monopoly of the major cola brands already on the market, Vaughan promoted her product not only at Miami street fairs like the Calle Ocho festival and Carnaval Miami, but also by purchasing advertising space on Ron Burkett's NASCAR racing car and by sponsoring a fishing contest at the Flora-Bama Lodge near Pensacola, in northwest Florida. She also crowned a "Miss Havana Cola" (a young woman who happened to be a Colombian). Her goal all along has been to broaden her company's base while retaining a Cuban identity.[6]

Hand in hand with economic success has come political involvement. When Cuban Americans began in the 1970s to win election to important judgeships, to the school board, and to city commissions, some Anglos fled north to Broward and Palm Beach counties.[7] By the 1990s, two young Cuban Americans had been elected to Congress—Ileana Ros-Lehtinen and Lincoln Díaz-Balart. Others have dominated city and county government in Miami-Dade and presided as mayor over the city of Miami and its separately administered surrounding county.

Cuban Americans who have succeeded in the mainstream of U.S. popular culture range from Desi Arnaz, a Hollywood and TV star in the 1940s and 1950s, to 1990s film stars Camerón Díaz, Andy García, María Conchita Alonso, and Steve Bauer. Lissette González, the 1997 Miss Carnaval de Miami (a contest for Cuban Americans), went on in 1998 to become Miss Florida and second runner-up for Miss America. The daughter of working-class parents (her father holds two jobs), she studied broadcast journalism and music at the University of Miami.

Mari Rodríguez Ichaso's emotional 1999 film about Cuban women in

Top left: Cuban American Lissette González performs at the Miss America talent competition. PHOTO: LISSETTE GONZÁLEZ

Top right: Lissette González with her parents, Arnaldo and Giselda González, at her crowning as Miss Florida 1998. She is the first Hispanic or Cuban American to win the state title. PHOTO: LISSETTE GONZÁLEZ

Left: Lissette González, Miss Florida, at Braman Honda, Bird Road, 1999. Cuban-born Norman Braman, one of González's sponsors, owns some of the largest automobile dealerships in South Florida. PHOTO: ROBERT M. LEVINE

exile, *Mujeres Cubanas: Marcadas por el Paraíso* (Cuban Women: Scarred by Paradise), portrays Cuban exiles converting nostalgia and suffering into a driving ambition. But Cuban American economic success in Miami (and elsewhere around the world) has come at a high price: the indifference of non-Cubans to the suffering of those who remain in Cuba. According to Luis Botifoll: "Despite their economic success, the Cubans continue to consider themselves as exiles. On the other hand, this success and their fight for a free Cuba has not won much sympathy from other Latin Americans and some Americans who resent what Cuban exiles have achieved."[8]

Miami may seem overwhelmingly Cuban, but it is home today to former residents from every Latin American country. As many as eighty thousand Brazilians live in South Florida, as well as tens of thousands of Haitians, Peruvians, and Jamaicans. Mexican farm workers toil in southern Miami-Dade County, in some cases in plant nurseries and fields owned by Cuban Americans. Large numbers of Venezuelans and Colombians have arrived as a consequence of political instability in their countries. Some of these immigrants have arrived as destitute as some of the first Cuban exiles; others, who came to the United States with assets and educations, live side by side with the Cuban American upper crust.

Moving up in the United States has for Cuban Americans in many cases meant moving on—fitting in so completely that today, for example, the largest and most successful Cuban radio stations are owned by non-Cuban Latins. Central Americans now run small shops even in Hialeah, which remains more than 90 percent Cuban American. Little Havana, where Cubans have been replaced mainly by Nicaraguans and other Central Americans, is now called by some Little Nicaragua.

Apartment building, Little Havana,

1989. Photo: Juan Carlos Espinosa

Community
and Religious Life

I n Cuba, family customs observed for generations changed or disappeared after Castro's takeover. The education system was revolutionized along with everything else. Catholic values and practices went by the board.

The regime manipulated family life as a form of social control. For example, hundreds of thousands of children were sent away from home—some even to the Soviet Union—to so-called fellowship (*becas*) schools for primary and secondary schooling. While the children had almost no contact with their parents for months at a time, the system indoctrinated them in Marxist-Leninist doctrines.

In Cuba today, it is not uncommon to find women and men who in their sixties have been legally married six to twelve times. Most of the marriages produced children, now often dispersed among family members in different parts of the island. When one marries in Cuba, one is permitted to buy special food to celebrate and to book rooms in hotels or at resorts—luxuries under the Castro regime that often enough justify divorcing and remarrying. Since Castro's revolution, abortion has become a common method of contraception.

Cubans indoctrinated in these customs who arrived in South Florida during the 1980 Mariel boat lift and since were bewildered when they found that many Cuban Americans still honored—at least to some degree—the traditional Cuban customs, celebrations, and codes of behavior. Especially among the early exile families, pre-1959 family values never changed. For them, the concept of family still extends to great-grandparents and great-grandchildren, to first cousins and second cousins, to godparents and their families, and to relatives-in-law.

On the whole, celebrations continue to be an important part of the Cuban American sense of family, including baby showers, baptisms, confirmations, bridal showers, and bachelor parties. In Miami, Thanksgiving, on

Havana Yacht Club organizational
meeting in exile, 1986. Many prominent
clubs from Cuba re-created themselves in
Miami. PHOTO: HISTORICAL MUSEUM OF
SOUTHERN FLORIDA

which day Cubans thank God for their united families and for the gift of living in freedom, has taken on the flavor of the Jewish Passover, a celebration of the liberation from Egyptian bondage. Nochebuena (Christmas Eve) is celebrated with equal verve by Catholic, secular, and other non-Catholic Cubans. The huge dinner on December 24 usually features roast pork, *yuca con mojo*, and rice and black beans. Cubans in Miami now exchange gifts on Christmas Day, replacing the traditional custom of giving gifts on the Día de los Reyes Magos (Three Kings' Day, or Epiphany).

At a Cuban American christening in Miami, parents will more often than not give their newborn a name popular in Cuba. ABC (American-born Cuban) girls frequently receive María as their first or middle name. Rarely do children receive American names such as Scott or Heather.

Kickball award ceremony at the Big Five Club, 1978. Each of the teams in the league was named for a Cuban club, among them the Havana Country Club and the Havana, Varadero, and Miramar yacht clubs. PHOTO: GARCÍA-VÉLEZ FAMILY

Winners of the 1985 Miami Rowing Club Regatta celebrate the seventy-fifth anniversary of the first race, held in Cuba. PHOTO: ROSA GUTIÉRREZ

Most Cuban American families continue to celebrate their daughters' fifteenth birthday—the Fiesta de Quince Años—even if they have to go into debt to do it. Traditionally, the *quince*, like the U.S. debut, announced not only the maturing of a daughter but the social importance of a family. But *quinceañera* customs have changed. Celebrations once limited to the Cuban community are now announced, with photographs, in the English-language press. "On August 18, 1998," one such announcement in the *Miami Herald* read, "our beautiful daughter Laura De Jesús celebrated her most waited fifteenth birthday, together with family and friends. A trip to Las Vegas followed."[1]

Cuban weddings differ from their U.S. counterparts in only a few ways. Often, while the bride and bridegroom are kneeling at the altar, a lace

Parking-lot smooch, 1999. Photo:
Robert M. Levine

mantilla is draped around their shoulders. Also, each receives a gift of five
brand-new coins to symbolize that as a couple they will be sharing their
material resources. Cuban American weddings are almost always religious
ceremonies, in contrast to those in Cuba, where most weddings are now
performed by civil authorities.

Funeral customs have remained traditional among Miami's Cubans.
Relatives and friends, in a show of respect for the deceased and the
deceased's family, prefer to remain close to the coffin all night and up to the
time for burial the next day. Some Cuban families became intensely angry
when they learned that Miami funeral homes closed at night and forced

A Cuban family's home, suburban Kendall, 1999. Neighbors often joke with the owners about the large numbers of cars parked on their lawn—sometimes as many as a dozen—during social get-togethers. PHOTO: ROBERT M. LEVINE

everyone to leave. The U.S. custom of a gathering after a burial where food and drink are served seems bizarre to most Cuban Americans.

To keep family ties strong, and for moral support, the early arrivals among the Cuban exiles clung to traditional moral values and insisted on them for their children. For example, when a Cuban American business-man's daughter, an average student at a Miami Roman Catholic prep school, wanted to attend college in the Northeast, the father (who arrived soon after Castro's takeover), a self-described "typical macho Cuban father," told her that she had to stay home until she married. "She agreed to stay in Miami," he said, "but made me promise that if her grades improved, she would

Cindy's birthday party, 1986. Cuban families make lavish parties to celebrate birthdays and other family events. Adults as well as children attend, often dancing into the night. Photo: Juan Carlos Espinosa

Cindy's birthday party, 1986. Photo: Juan Carlos Espinosa

A clown joins the guests at the buffet table at Cindy's party, 1986. Photo: Juan Carlos Espinosa

Shrine in front of a private home,
Hialeah, 1999. PHOTO: ROBERT M. LEVINE

transfer. She did very well during her first year, so I permitted her to transfer to American University. After three days, she called us, telling us that she
wanted to come home. She finished college and law school in Miami." Boys
were less restricted, although it took some doing to convince Cuban parents
to permit their sons to attend the University of Florida in Gainesville, a half
day's drive north of Miami.

Among the early arriving exiles, well-connected families sent their children to schools where Spanish was spoken. The bilingual private education
sector not only benefited economically itself from the influx of new students
but offered the Cuban exiles schooling for their children that would empha-
size their heritage. Among these schools were the Conchita Espinosa Academy, the Edison School, Carrollton School for Girls, St. Brendan's, and Belén
Jesuit Academy. Students of college age attended Villanueva University
(renamed St. Thomas in Miami) and Barry College, a Catholic institution

Under the birthday-party piñata, Kendall, 1979. If this three-year-old girl lived in Cuba, at age seven she would be asked to join the Communist Pioneers. Her teachers would tell her that she must choose between being "God's daughter" or "Fidel's daughter." PHOTO: GARCÍA-VÉLEZ FAMILY

Girls outside St. Brendan's Church before their first communion, 1979.

Immaculate Conception School graduation class, 1959.

Quince party, 1976, the traditional celebration of a girl's fifteenth birthday. PHOTO: HISTORICAL MUSEUM OF SOUTHERN FLORIDA

Dancing at a quince party. Among Miami Cubans, the traditional lavish party for the quinceañera is giving way to vacation trips or other forms of celebration. PHOTO: PATRICIA GARCÍA-VÉLEZ

for girls that for decades had attracted students from Latin America. Other affluent Cuban exile families enrolled their children in such private schools as Lourdes Academy, Ransom-Everglades (the most prestigious prep school in Miami), and Palmer-Trinity, and such Roman Catholic schools as Christopher Columbus, LaSalle, and St. Hugh's.

Yet even the modest tuition charged by these schools was too high for

Graduation from Our Lady of Lourdes Academy, 1996. The school is a member of the Bilingual Private Schools Association in Miami, founded in 1975, which included several other schools directly transplanted from Cuba: the Ruston Academy, Champagnat Catholic Schools, the Edison School, and Baldor School. Those with English names had the same names in Cuba. PHOTO: GARCÍA-VÉLEZ FAMILY

Maggie Díaz and Eduardo Sierra's wedding ceremony at the Immaculate Conception Parish, 1972. The pastor is Father Gustavo Miyares, the bride's father's nephew. PHOTO: RAFAEL DÍAZ FAMILY

Carmen de Cárdenas and Calixto García-Vélez marry in the Church of the Little Flower, Coral Gables, 1994. The mantilla, a lace shawl, is traditionally draped over the bride and groom's shoulders to symbolize their union. PHOTO: ALBERTO ROMEU

Praying at St. Lazarus's Shrine, East Hialeah, 1987. The most popular saint in Cuba, San Lázaro is a Cuban creation with no roots in Christian liturgy. PHOTO: JUAN CARLOS ESPINOSA

Repairing St. Lazarus's arm, 1999. Afro-Cuban cults became widespread in Miami after Mariel. Botánicas supply statues, plant extracts, seeds, leaves, food, and all paraphernalia for Santería practitioners. Santería originated in West Africa and was brought to the New World by slaves, but in recent decades Cubans of all social classes have been attracted to it. Among many, though, it is socially unacceptable because it involves animal sacrifice and possession by spirits. Nonetheless, babalawos (cult leaders) offer confidential advice that gives self-assurance. PHOTO: ROBERT M. LEVINE

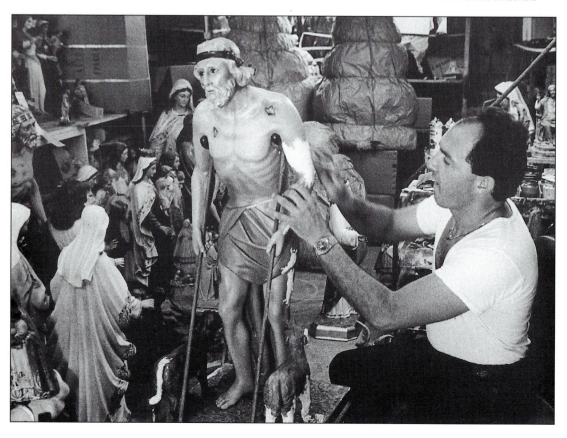

Saints in religious shop, Little Havana, 1999. In 1967, Little Havana's San Juan Bosco Church inaugurated a program to offer Catholic instruction and Cuban history to elementary and secondary students enrolled in the public schools.

PHOTO: ROBERT M. LEVINE

most newly arriving exile families. They sent their children to public schools, where for the most part they were not welcomed by an educational system that managed to remain inflexible and condescending at the same time it was struggling to keep up with their numbers. Over time, the Hialeah and Little Havana public schools became overwhelmingly Cuban American. By the mid-1990s, this pattern had changed. The economic success of a growing number of Cuban Americans carried them to wealthier communities, with mixed school attendance patterns that reflected their improved standard of living.

Regardless of their income level, most of Miami's Cuban Americans

Spanish evangelical church, Little Havana, 1999. In Miami, evangelical Protestant denominations have attracted many Cubans, especially those who came after 1980 and who therefore lacked Roman Catholic upbringing. Presbyterians and other evangelicals helped arriving exiles from the early 1960s onward. Some Cubans belonged to Baptist, Methodist, and Presbyterian churches in Cuba, but fewer, with the exception of Jehovah's Witnesses, were Pentecostals. Photo: Robert M. Levine

retain close ties with their extended family members. (The García-Vélez family, for example, purchased ten acres of land in Kendall and built ten houses for family members—all sharing a common backyard.) Togetherness and family loyalty are expressed in frequent phone calls and in Sunday gatherings, usually at the parents' home, for lunch, considered the most important meal of the week. (One tradition that disappeared quickly

Testimonial at a spiritist meeting, Hialeah, 1986. Spiritists, who represent only a small portion of Cubans in South Florida, are highly devoted to their rituals.

PHOTO: JUAN CARLOS ESPINOSA

among Miami's Cubans, as in Cuba itself, was the inclusion in such gatherings of the family's priest, physician, and attorney, and the reliance on them for close counsel.)

The tables at these family feasts groan under dishes of *arroz con pollo* (saffron rice cooked with chicken and mixed with beer, tomatoes, red peppers, peas, garlic, and onions); of *plátanos chatinos* (green plantains fried in lard and then pressed and refried), ripe fried plantains, *yuca con mojo* (a mix of onion, garlic, sour orange juice, and lemon juice cooked in olive oil), and *ajiaco* (a souplike casserole made of taro, yuca, sweet potato, white potato, green plantain, corncob, pork, chicken, meat, blood sausage, and hard pork sausage). Salads of tomato, cucumber, lettuce, red pepper, and other vegetables dressed with olive oil and vinegar are passed around. Favorite beverages include iced beer or Pepsi. Alcohol consumption has progressively declined as more and more people have needed to drive home, rather than walk. Adherence to traditional menus, too, is not as nearly universal now as it was forty years ago. The family lunch might be a barbecue.

Perhaps the spirit of Miami Cubans regarding cultural customs is best

Cartoon: "The Cuban Revolution as a Biblical Parable," by José M. Varela. (1) In the Beginning: In Cuba, there was everything . . . then it became nothing. (2) Adam and Eve: And paradise was created with its forbidden fruit. (Eve: "I got this by being a hooker.") (3) Cain and Abel: Then the militiaman denounced his brother the worm . . . but later he was pardoned in Hialeah. (Abel: "Now you want me to lend you money?" Cain: "I've run out of food stamps.") (4) Noah's Ark: When things got worse, they built a giant raft. (5) The Tower of Babel: And thus the people started to speak different languages. (6) Moses [Fidel]: leading his tribe for 40 years. ("Sooner or later manna will fall from heaven.") (7) The Twelve Apostles: Stuck fundraising for the cause at the Last Supper [Victor's Cafe was a popular Miami Cuban restaurant]. (8) The Last Judgment: (Angel: "[Singer Willy] Chirino says that he's coming." Devil: "Get down from that cloud!") . . . But those who became American citizens were saved.

captured by the comments of several members of the Hogaristas in Exile, an alumni association of 637 former students of Havana's Escuela del Hogar, a school for young ladies. The school taught its students "to love [their] country and take pride in raising a family and to go on to make a life for [them]selves," explains Yolanda Seamann, a Hogarista.

"Tradition is the soul of a country," said another, Emma Cotarelo de Milián. "Even though I was forced to leave my country, I can still share those traditions with my children and my community."[2]

The Arts and Politics

I F WHAT MAKES ART and what makes good art are matters of taste, what makes good Cuban and Cuban American art has often been a matter of both taste and politics.

The satiric songs of Cuban *cantautor* (songwriter and performer) Pedro Luis Ferrer touch on subjects ranging from racism to homophobia to the privileges of the elite. In March 1999 Ferrer received an enthusiastic response at a University of Miami concert, part of a tour arranged by his recording agent. Ten years earlier, the same concert might have been canceled or picketed, because Ferrer is popular in Cuba and lives there.

But popular Cuban American singer Gloria Estefan has complained about the continued hostility toward Cuban artists. "I cannot imagine how we could explain to the people of Cuba," she wrote in a letter to the *Miami Herald*, "that the very freedoms that they so desperately desire and deserve are being annihilated in their name." The letter brought Estefan harsh criticism from many Cuban Americans in Florida.

Even the choices the exiles make about what music to listen to can

Singer Willy Chirino at Carnaval de la Calle Ocho, 1985. Chirino's wife came to the United States on a Pedro Pan flight.

PHOTO: MAX LESNICK COLLECTION

Second-hand romance novels, Little Havana, 1989. Dozens of Spanish bookstores have flourished in Miami, including La Moderna Poesía, Cervantes, Universal, and Impacto. PHOTO: JUAN CARLOS ESPINOSA

become political. Before the 1970s, Cuban music—enormously popular among the exiles—consisted entirely of old standbys. Most of the well-known Cuban musicians of the late 1950s remained on the island, so playing these old songs revived the popularity of singers and groups of the previous generation. "When I was growing up in Miami in the early 1960s," Gustavo Pérez-Firmat remembers, "we heard resistance music. What we were resisting was the reality of exile. At once reticent and self-indulgent, this music had a dual purpose, for it allowed one to vent the affect of exile— the nostalgia and the disorientation and the sorrow—without directly confronting its specific circumstances."[1] Albums one could buy in Little

Cartoon by Silvio Fontanellas. Although more than 60 percent of Cuba's population today is black or mulatto, only a tiny percentage of Cubans in Miami are blacks. Many dark-skinned Cubans preferred to settle in New York and New Jersey or in such countries as Mexico, Angola, and Mozambique. PHOTO: UNIVERSITY OF MIAMI SPECIAL COLLECTIONS

Monument to Cuban Culture, Hialeah, 1999. Markers and monuments in this waterfront park, created in 1990, commemorate giants of Cuban popular culture in exile. PHOTO: ROBERT M. LEVINE

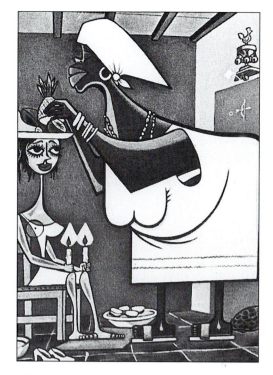

George Sánchez, 1999, with visitors at his Bay of Pigs art exhibit, "Monumento," Coconut Grove. The inflated pink pig, along with the rest of the exhibition, was destroyed by unidentified vandals two days after the photo was taken. PHOTO: ROBERT M. LEVINE

Poster from George Sánchez's Bay of Pigs exhibit, 1999. POSTCARD: GEORGE SÁNCHEZ

Statue of José Martí, downtown Miami, 1999. Every January 28, schoolchildren decorate the site with flowers. PHOTO: ROBERT M. LEVINE

Havana, he remembers, had names like *Cuba de Ayer* (Cuba of Yesteryear) and *Nostalgia de Cuba* (Nostalgia for Cuba).

By the 1970s, the younger members of exile families, at least, were ready for a new message. The popularity of Cuban exile singers in Miami was on the rise. Willy Chirino began recording in 1974. Born in Cuba in 1942, he finished high school in Miami, then started a rock band. For a few years, Willy Chirino and the Windjammers were in demand at South Florida hotels and resorts. The next big Cuban American success came in 1977—the Miami Sound Machine, with singer Gloria Estefan.

The message of the new popular musicians was not "when I left Cuba," but "we're here—and we're celebrating our heritage in our new culture." A

Cartoon: "History of Cuba" by José M. Varela. (1) Many years ago, Cubans lived on their island, smoked cigars, and talked garbage. (2) The Spanish tourists came and took over the island, its tobacco, and its hookers. (3) In addition, musicians and athletes were brought over from Africa. (5) Once independent, Cubans began to build the greatest republic in the world. (6) But then came the Commander [Fidel], who turned things upside down. (7) And thus Cubans are worse off than ever—and they can't even talk garbage. Throughout the cartoon, the dialogue is equally sarcastic: (5) "Have we become more developed than the Americans?" "At least from the waist down"; (6) Fidel: "From now on, you're going to work more than the Germans and eat less than the Somalis."

new radio station, Super Q (WQBA) popularized this new local Cuban music and appealed to the younger Cuban American market. In the 1980s, the tastes of these young Miamians broadened to include the recorded music from Cuba that had begun to filter into their community despite the embargo. Older Cuban exiles still tuned to AM radio, with its talk shows and soap operas and old-fashioned Cuban music.[2] In the familiar tunes they found the "imagined Havana"—some say that for many older Cubans, an imagined Havana is what Miami still represents.

Even Cubans raised in the United States have found overwhelming the nostalgic pull of the island that music can create. "I cry when I hear the

Cuban National Anthem," says Cuban American Pulitzer Prize–winning journalist Liz Balmaseda, "although I came here when I was only ten months old."[3]

But Gloria Estefan's plea for artistic acceptance did not apply only to musicians. Paintings and other visual art produced by Cubans continue to draw hostility, particularly those produced by Cubans living on the island. At an auction held at Miami's Cuban Museum of Art on April 22, 1988, José Juara, a member of Brigade 2506, successfully bid $500 for a painting, *El Pavo Real*, by the flamboyant Cuban artist Manuel Mendive. Juara then took the painting outside and, in the presence of five hundred people, set it aflame. Miami city commissioners voted not to renew the museum's lease. Although subsequent attempts to evict the museum were thwarted by the courts, it finally closed down. Juara's action was a political statement. As he explained eleven years later, "I burned that painting because I foresaw the ideological penetration from communist Cuba that was beginning to take place in the Cuban exile community."[4]

Cuban American painters in the United States have been told that to sell their work they must either adopt an "international" style to sidestep being Cuban or paint naive Santería scenes—a suggestion that stems from the stereotypes non-Cubans have about Cuban culture. Artist George Sánchez, who grew up in New York City and Miami, relates that people told him, "You're not really Cuban—you are an American. Get over being Cuban." Sánchez responded, he says, with exasperation. "I am Cuban. Miami is Cuba. Cuba is now a third-world country."[5]

On April 17, 1999, Sánchez mounted an exhibit of his art in the Coconut Grove airplane hangar where Brigade veterans from the Bay of Pigs had been welcomed after they were freed. He used an inflated pink pig as well as photographs of participants and tiny airplanes to invoke the memory of the

"No Castro No Problem." The
emblematic slogan of Cuban exile politics.
PHOTO: ROBERT M. LEVINE

tragedy. Although he had designed the exhibit to raise the consciousness of
Cuban Americans of his generation, Sánchez received anonymous threat-
ening telephone calls from people opposed to his depiction of the invasion.
On the fifth day of the exhibit, Sánchez arrived at the hanger to find his
exhibit vandalized so badly that he was forced to close it.

Yet in the late 1990s, at least some musicians and artists who live in Cuba
were making regular appearances in Miami. Post-1959 Cuban-made films,
once denounced and boycotted, are shown regularly to appreciative audi-
ences in local film festivals.

When new paintings by Manuel Mendive were displayed at a Miami
gallery in Coral Gables in April 1999, no one tried to burn them. The exhibit
caused no incident at all.

José Tonito Rodríguez is the founder of the Bridge of Cuban Artists, a 500-member organization. He came to Miami in 1980 (he is now thirty-seven) and has traveled back to the island twice to take photographs to explain his childhood to his U.S.-born sons. Rodríguez admitted in an early 1999 interview that in days past, when he drove his 1968 Mustang convertible around Miami, he turned down the volume on Havana-based musicians like Los Van Van or Silvio Rodríguez. He told the journalist he "[didn't] want to offend anyone." But "now I just crank it up—and nobody cares."[6]

Yet in October 1999, when thousands flocked to a Los Van Van concert in the Miami Arena, small groups of angry protestors had to be held in check by police. The *Miami Herald* for October 15 reported the reaction of Democracy Movement leader Ramón Saúl Sánchez, convicted in the late 1970s for anti-Castro terrorist acts, who spoke out against the protestors' violence and obscenities: "Sadly, the peaceful demonstration that it was supposed to be soon became tainted by the acts of a group of people who began to throw rocks, cans and other objects, contradicting the goals of the demonstrations and the peaceful and democratic principles of most of those who attended."

Añorada Cuba Place, Hialeah, 1999. *Añorada* means nostalgia, deep emotional affection. The street was renamed following a festival at that location honoring Cuban culture. Photo: Moisés Asís

"Dreaming about the Island"

M Y FATHER STRUGGLED with the idea of departure from the place that had been his home for thirty-five years," explains a young Cuban American, "and with the thought of leaving his hardearned possessions behind," including his car, his business, and two parcels of land he had bought for investment and on which he had planned to build a new home for his family. In fact, because he was convinced that "Castro's days were numbered," he stayed behind, sending his daughters ahead. When he and his wife did leave the island, in June 1962, "the Cuban authorities carefully inventoried all of his belongings, everything except his prized gold watch, which he entrusted to a friend, vowing to be back." When he arrived at Miami International Airport, his daughter "was struck by how much he seemed to have aged. His thinning hair, now completely gray, was a first indication of [his] trauma."

"Although my mother found a completely menial job," the young woman added, "having to work afforded her a self-confidence and an independence that she had never known under my father's strict tutelage." Her father died some years later, never returning to Cuba or recovering his watch.[1]

Some exiles never adjusted to life off the island.

Many Cubans were literally erased from the official history of their homeland. Writers and scholars who left had their published books removed from libraries, making them "nonpersons" in the Orwellian language of apartheid South Africa and Stalin's Soviet Union. Everyone who left Cuba— a country with a rich history of patriotic pride—was branded a traitor.[2]

Miami Cubans often have nightmares about leaving Cuba. One man describes frightening dreams in which he has returned to the island to visit relatives but is robbed of his documents and detained at the airport when he tries to fly home. Or he dreams of when he was seventeen and in prison;

Home off Bird Road, Coral Gables, 1999, displays the Cuban coat of arms.

PHOTO: PATRICIA GARCÍA-VÉLEZ

Former Madruga journalist José Valera at home in Little Havana, 1999. The Valeras, who had lived in Madrid and New York, came to South Florida in 1974 "because Miami was so close to Cuba."

PHOTO: ROBERT M. LEVINE

one of the other inmates, his pal, was the only survivor of a small group of teenagers who had tried to flee by hiding in the tires of an Iberia airlines plane—the rest froze or fell into the ocean. Or he dreams he is crossing a minefield, trying to get into Guantanamo. He wakes up in panic: "Am I in Miami or in Cuba?" Once he assures himself he is safely in Florida, he falls back to sleep.

Not only the nightmares but also the intensity of anti-Castro feelings keep Cuba alive in Miami. Cuban Americans thrive on myths, gossip, and rumors about Castro. For instance, it is widely (and erroneously) believed that, as a young man, he was offered a professional baseball contract by the Washington Senators—had he signed, there would have been no revolution. Rumors that Castro is suffering from a terminal disease, or has died, often sweep through the city.

Gustavo Pérez-Firmat explains the exiles' state in the early years:

Nourishment as well as narcotic, news from Cuba jolted us, made us buzz with anticipation, fed our hopes and blunted our frustrations. All of this gossip helped us cope with exile, but it also diminished our need to move beyond it. Perhaps if we had been less prone to wishful thinking, we would have paid more attention to the American here and now; but instead, here and now collapsed into nowhere, and we lived dreaming about the island across the water.[3]

With the passage of the years, the exiles' expectations of Castro's demise and of their own return to the island have faded to hope, and hope has given way to nostalgia. "I'm nostalgic because I have to be," joked Cuban American playwright Carmen Peláez. "I wear a black bra," one of her characters mocked, "because I am mourning the death of my country."[4]

Food-selling booth, Feria de los Municipios de Cuba en el Exilio (Exile Municipalities Fair), 1999. The fair, held annually in the vast parking lot of the Flagler Dog Track, attracts thousands of visitors each year. PHOTO: ROBERT M. LEVINE

La Habana (Havana) booth, Feria de los Municipios de Cuba en el Exilio (Exile Municipalities Fair), 1999. Most Cuban cities have fair booths, which serve typical meals as well as a good deal of beer. Friends from the old days come by and chat. PHOTO: ROBERT M. LEVINE

Yet Cubans retain enormous pride in their heritage. "Being Cuban is contagious!" one Cuban American observed. Cubanía is taught to new generations in many cases by telling children that they are different from other Latin Americans, from all other immigrants, and that they are equal to or better than Americans in intelligence and work skills. At home, children are taught to speak Spanish, to study hard, and to remember Cuba's beautiful history of bravery and sacrifice. Despite the Batista regime's putting an end to democracy, children are told, Cuba before Castro was one of the best countries in the world in which to live.

Most of the younger patrons of Café Nostalgia, a Miami nightclub opened in 1996 by former Havana film director "Pepe" Horta, have never set

Feria de los Municipios de Cuba en el Exilio (Exile Municipalities Fair), 1999. "Going back to Cuba now," a patron of one booth said, "would be like returning to a dream." PHOTO: ROBERT M. LEVINE

The Guantanamo booth, Feria de los Municipios de Cuba en el Exilio (Exile Municipalities Fair), 1999. PHOTO: ROBERT M. LEVINE

foot on Cuban soil. With other Cuban Americans, they come together to watch old black-and-white movies and listen to Cuban music. Why cling to their family's culture? Twenty-year-old Flory Méndez answers, "I guess it's in my blood." "Our role," another says, "is to serve as a bridge between Miami and Havana."[5]

Some young upwardly mobile Cuban Americans lay claim to their heritage by calling themselves YUCAs (Young Urban Cuban Americans). The acronym is a play on the word *yuca*, a garlicky, starchy tuber that appears in popular Cuban dishes, often served with *congrí* (rice and beans) and meat or chicken.

The personal experience of Peter Sánchez, a professor at Loyola

Admiring a 1959 Cadillac with a vintage Havana license plate, Cuba Nostalgia Exposition, 1999. PHOTO: ROBERT M. LEVINE

Cuba Nostalgia Exposition, 1999. Cubans come to look for their old neighborhoods on a map of pre-1959 Havana. PHOTO: ROBERT M. LEVINE

University in Chicago, is telling. As a youth, he Anglicized his name, Pedro, and tried hard to distance himself from his Cuban roots. During the past decade, which included a trip to the island in 1995, his perspective has changed. "I have been slowly but surely retaking my heritage," he writes. "I now proudly say that I am Cuban or Cuban-American. There was a time when I would not say that."[6]

But if Castro did topple, polls show, only 30 percent of Miami's Cuban Americans say that they would move back to the island. The rest, like the exiles who arrived in Miami without baggage and often without even birth certificates, hold their Cuba in their minds and hearts.

The Power of Nostalgia

THE EXILE," writes Ricardo Pau-Llosa, "knows his place, and that place is the imagination."[1] Not so for most Cuban exiles in Miami: through hard work and entrepreneurship, they created a community life that was vibrant and very real.

Over the years, Cuban American families have adapted U.S. customs while retaining an outlook uniquely Cuban in flavor. They read American newspapers but often take not the *Miami Herald* but the Spanish-language

Cuban Independence Day, May 20, 1985. On May 20, 1902, the United States ended its occupation of Cuba and returned to Cubans the independence for which they had fought bravely for thirty years. PHOTO: HISTORICAL MUSEUM OF SOUTHERN FLORIDA

Mural over the altar in the Ermita de la Caridad, the Chapel of Our Lady of Charity, Cuba's patron saint, 1999. The chapel sits next to Mercy Hospital and LaSalle High School on the edge of Biscayne Bay, facing south toward Cuba. The mural depicts a rich mixture of figures from Cuban history: Columbus, Bartolomé de las Casas, José Martí, Mariana Grajales (the mother of the Maceo brothers), Máximo Gómez, and dozens of bishops and archbishops. For Cubans, Our Lady of Charity is not only the mother of Jesus but the symbol of Cuba's hopes and aspirations. PHOTO: ROBERT M. LEVINE

View of Biscayne Bay outside Ermita de la Caridad (Our Lady of Charity Chapel), facing south toward Cuba, 1999.
PHOTO: ROBERT M. LEVINE

"Sing, Don't Cry" mural on Southwest 8th Street, Little Havana, 1999. The man with the cigar wears a "Generation Ñ" T-shirt. On the far right are the "Spy vs. Spy" cartoon characters, popularized via *Mad* magazine during the cold war era.
PHOTO: ROBERT M. LEVINE

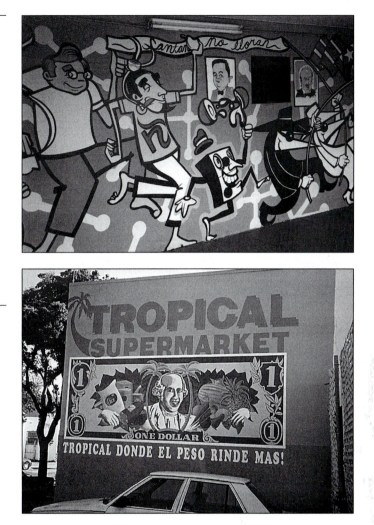

Hand-painted mural at a Tropical Supermarket parking lot, Little Havana, 1999. PHOTO: ROBERT M. LEVINE

El Nuevo Herald. More than a translation of the English-language version, it carries considerably more coverage of Cuban American and Cuban events, and in that way is more like the *Diario de las Américas.*

Along with American publications, Cubans buy a wide variety of exile tabloids (*periodiquitos*), and magazines like *Vanidades,* a cross between *Vogue* and *People.*

In the early 1980s, some of Miami's Cuban American stations altered their programming to appeal to Cuban youth, playing American rock music as well as Cuban standards.[2] In 1994, there were three hardline Cuban radio stations; five years later, only two remain, WAQI (Radio Mambí) and

The Santa Bárbara *fritanga* (cafeteria), Little Havana, 1999, caters to its new, mostly Nicaraguan, clientele along with its longtime customers. Since the mid-1990s, Little Havana has been increasingly transformed into Little Nicaragua, as civil wars in Central America drive thousands of immigrants and refugees to Miami.

PHOTO: ROBERT M. LEVINE

WWFE (La Poderosa). The other Cuban stations—including WQBA, Radio Fé, Radio Progreso—are less political. Cuban flags, before 1985 flown from thousands of Cuban homes and businesses in Miami, have become a rare sight.

A longtime human rights activist who came to Miami in the mid-1990s found that some ardently anti-Castro and anti-Communist exiles there had made big profits not only by doing business with Communist and antidemocratic regimes around the world, but sometimes by using child labor and maintaining terrible conditions for workers. "Some Cubans owning businesses and factories treat their employees terribly, providing deplorable working conditions and firing those who complain," she said. "I thought, poor Cuba, if her future is in the hands of Cubans like those!"[3]

She also complained that professionals from Cuba who have defected to South Florida relatively recently are offered by Cuban Americans jobs that no one else will take. Often even in these jobs, they are paid less than non-Hispanic entry-level workers, even those with no experience.

When the Clinton administration sent up a trial balloon in late January 1999 suggesting that the United States open the door to increased relations with Cuba, protests by Cuban Americans came mostly from the older generation. The Cuban American community has substantially changed, not in terms of pride in or attachment to Cuban customs, but in the thinking of the newer generations. Members of Generation Ñ (pronounced "enyey"), made up of the children of Cuban exiles and the newer arrivals, still support the embargo, but they lack the tenacious resolve of Alpha 66 and Jorge Mas Canosa (dead of cancer in 1997) to resist unconditionally the thought of some level of U.S. recognition of the Castro government. There is a greater sense of openness.

Miami retains a concrete record of Cuban influence evident even to the passing eye. Many Miami businesses and institutions have preserved their old Cuban names. Miami's Bell South Yellow Pages in 1999 listed 279 entries (businesses and institutions) that include the word "Cuba" or "Cuban." An additional 120 include "Havana" or "Habana"; 31 more include "Varadero," the name of Cuba's most famous beach. Many other entries contain the names of other Cuban cities and towns, among them Matanzas, Pinar del Río, Camagüey, Holguín, Baracoa. Others have names from Cuban's Indian

Cartoon: "Exile Life, Miami Style" by José M. Varela. This light-hearted tribute to the stubbornness of the Cuban exile generation depicts an unshaven guajiro relaxing at his hut in the middle of the "New Miami." The city offers all the accoutrements of modern life, including, in the lower corners of the drawing, a condom and a syringe.

heritage: Taíno, Cacique, Bohío. Many retail shops have taken the hallowed names of stores in Cuba, names no longer found on the island.

Dozens of Miami streets are named for heroes of Cuban history and culture, even though most of the city's streets have numbers rather than names. They can walk along José Martí Street and Máximo Gómez Avenue; streets named for anti-Castro martyrs (Pedro Luis Boitel and Tony Cuesta), businessmen (Luis Sabines, Nathan Rok, and Felipe Vals), singers (Celia Cruz, Olga Guillot), bankers (Carlos Arboleya and Abel Holtz), athletes (José Canseco), poets (Ernesto Montaner), and lawyers (Carlos B. Fernández). Añorada Cuba Place in Hialeah translates as "Beloved Cuba," and there is a Cuban Cultural Heritage Place nearby.

In Miami, but not in Havana, you can buy a "Cuban sandwich" and "Cuban bread," Bacardi rum and Hatuey beer. The city is once again home to Cuban social clubs, municipal governments in exile, a Cuban American beauty pageant, and Cuban trade and professional organizations.

To be sure, there is no monolithic Cuban American community in Miami, and there never has been. Every Cuban American in South Florida has adjusted in a unique way, borne of origin, circumstance, experience, and luck. The achievements of Miami's Cuban exiles and their descendants in South Florida are no figment of anyone's imagination.

They are real, and they are lasting.

Introduction

1. Louis A. Pérez, *Cuba: Between Reform and Revolution* (New York: Oxford University Press, 1988), 13.
2. Alejandro Portes and Robert L. Bach, *Latin Journey: Cuban and Mexican Immigrants in the United States* (Berkeley: University of California Press, 1985), 84.
3. Ibid.
4. María Cristina García, *Havana USA: Cuban Exiles and Cuban Americans in South Florida, 1959–1994* (Berkeley: University of California Press, 1996), 85.
5. Angel Tomás González, *Cambio* (Madrid), vol. 16, "Gusanos Patriotas," March 22, 1994.
6. See Luis J. Botifoll, *Cómo se creó la nueva imagen de Miami* (Miami: Consejo Nacional Cubano de Planificación, 1984).
7. Ibid.
8. See Dorita Roca Mariña, "A Theoretical Discussion of What Changes and What Stays the Same in Cuban Immigrant Families," in José Szapocznik and María Cristina Herrera, eds., *Cuban Americans: Acculturation, Adjustment, and the Family* (Washington, D.C.: National Coalition of Hispanic Mental Health and Human Services Organizations, 1978).

Old Miami

1. Other indigenous peoples had inhabited South Florida as far back as twelve thousand years ago. See Von N. Beebe and William F. Mackey, *Bilingual Schooling and the Miami Experience* (Coral Gables: GSIS, 1990), 15–16; Arva Moore Parks and Gregory W. Bush, *Miami: The American Crossroad* (Coral Gables: University of Miami Institute for Public History, 1996), 2.
2. Miguel González-Pando, *The Cuban Americans* (Westport, Conn.: Greenwood Press, 1998), 1; Alejandro Portes and Alex Stepick, *City on the Edge: The Transformation of Miami* (Berkeley: University of California Press, 1993), 67–69.
3. See Rolando Alvarez Estévez, *La Emigración Cubana en Estados Unidos, 1868–1878* (Havana, 1986).
4. Portes and Stepick, *City on the Edge*, 63–67.
5. See Louis A. Pérez Jr., *Cuba: Between Reform and Revolution* (New York: Oxford University Press, 1988), 205.
6. Portes and Stepick, *City on the Edge*, 97.
7. *Guía de Miami: La Ciudad Mágica*, vol. 4 (1946); *Directorio de Miami/ Miami Beach, Edición de 1951* (1951).

The Politics of Dislocation

1. Cited by Pérez, *Cuba*, 321.
2. Interview, Miami, March 6, 1999. The interviewee asked to remain anonymous.
3. García, *Havana USA*, 16–17.
4. Msgr. Bryan O. Walsh, interviewed by Patricia García-Vélez, May 22, 1999.
5. Curiously, in Cuba the airlift is called "Peter Pan," while in Miami many Cubans call it "Pedro Pan."
6. García, *Havana USA*, 19.
7. The events of this period are concisely summarized by González-Pando, *The Cuban Americans*, 17–30.
8. See Thomas D. Boswell and James R. Curtis, *The Cuban-American Experience: Culture, Images, and Perspectives* (Totowa, N.J.: Rowan & Allenheld, 1983), ch. 10.
9. Ibid., 7.
10. See Aleksandr Fursenko and Timothy Naftali, *One Hell of a Gamble* (New York: Norton, 1997), 327.
11. González-Pando, *The Cuban Americans*, 52.
12. Portes and Bach, *Latin Journey*, 85–86; Boswell and Curtis, *The Cuban-American Experience*, 44–48.
13. Boswell and Curtis, *The Cuban-American Experience*, 48–49.

Marielitos and Rafters

1. Portes and Stepick, *City on the Edge*, 20–21; Portes and Bach, *Latin Journey*, 86–87.
2. *Time*, May 19, 1980, 14–15.
3. Piedad Bucholtz, quoted in Helga Silva, "The Children of Mariel" (Washington, D.C.: Cuban American National Foundation, 1985), 16.
4. Portes and Stepick, *City on the Edge*, 32, 36.
5. E-mail, José M. Szapocznik to Robert M. Levine, June 3, 1999.
6. García, *Havana USA*, 118.
7. Pérez, *Cuba*, 398–399.
8. Alejandro Portes, "Morning in Miami: A New Era for Cuban-American Politics," *PLAS Bulletin*, Princeton University (Fall 1998), 1–2.
9. Rafael Hernández, *Relaciones Cuba-Emigración Cubana, 1978–1994* (Havana: Edición Sección de

Información Científica–Centro de Estudios Sobre América, 1994), n.p.; García, *Havana USA*, 78–79.

10. See Félix Masud-Piloto, *From Welcome Exiles to Illegal Immigrants* (Lanham, Md.: Rowan & Littlefield, 1996); Holly Ackerman and Juan M. Clark, *The Cuban Balseros: Voyage of Uncertainty* (Miami: Policy Center of the Cuban-American National Council, 1995), 35–39; García, *Havana USA*, ix.

11. "The Sounds of Spanglish," *Hopscotch* 1:1 (1999), 161–171. See the forthcoming pocket guide by Bill Cruz, *The Official Spanglish Dictionary* (New York: Fireside Press, 1999).

12. Susana Bellido, "A Rarity Today," *Miami Herald*, March 31, 1999.

The Flavors of Transition

1. González-Pando, *The Cuban Americans*, 50.

2. Ibid., 42–43, 55–56.

3. Gustavo Pérez-Firmat, *Life on the Hyphen: The Cuban-American Way* (Austin: University of Texas Press, 1994), 8.

Fitting In

1. Gustavo Pérez-Firmat, *Next Year in Cuba*, 54–55, cited by Ricardo Castells, "Next Year in Cuba: Gustavo Pérez-Firmat and the Rethinking of the Cuban-American Experience," *SECOLAS Annals* 30:3 (1999), 30.

2. See José Llanes, *Cuban Americans: Masters of Survival* (Cambridge, Mass.: Aby Books, 1982), 185.

3. Ibid., 186.

4. García, *Havana USA*, 90.

5. Boswell and Curtis, *The Cuban-American Experience*, 86.

6. "Cristina," as told to Robert M. Levine, March 10, 1999.

7. Efraín Veiga, quoted by Mireya Navarro, "Cubans in Miami," *New York Times*, February 11, 1999.

Moving Up

1. See González-Pando, *The Cuban Americans*, 33–36.

2. Interview, May 15, 1999. The interviewee asked to remain anonymous.

3. Navarro, "Cubans in Miami."

4. CAC "United Health Care Plans of Florida," Company Overview, Miami, 1998. Courtesy of Mary Lorenzo.

5. See Miami-Dade web site; www.odci.gov/cia/publications/factbook/cu.html (the *CIA Factbook*).

6. Kathy Glasgow, "Soda Jerked," *New Times*, April 29–May 5, 1999, 7, 9.

7. Navarro, "Cubans in Miami."

8. Luis J. Botifoll, statement to Moisés Asís, June 4, 1999.

Community and Religious Life

1. *Miami Herald*, April 4, 1999.

2. Cited by Tere Figueras, *Miami Herald*, April 29, 1999, Neighbors section.

The Arts and Politics

1. Pérez-Firmat, *Life on the Hyphen*, 104.

2. Ibid., 107–115.

3. Paraphrased from Liz Balmaseda's statement in Mari Rodríguez Ichaso's documentary, *Mujeres Cubanas: Marcadas por el Paraíso*.

4. Quoted by Lissette Corsa, "Art to Burn," *New Times*, April 8–14, 1999, 7–8.

5. George Sánchez, interview with authors, April 18, 1999.

6. Quoted on the Internet www.newsweek.com/nw~srv/printed/int/wa/ovin0103_4.htm, February 2, 1999.

"Dreaming about the Island"

1. Rosa Perelmuter, "From Havana to Hub: Two Cuban-Jewish Responses to Exile" ms., 1–5, courtesy of the author.

2. Yolanda Martínez-San Miguel, "Cuban Migration Today," *PLAS Bulletin*, Princeton University (Fall 1998), 3.

3. Pérez-Firmat, *Next Year in Cuba*, 77, cited by Castells, "Next Year in Cuba."

4. Carmen Peláez, *Rum & Coke*, performance at the University of Miami, April 8, 1999.

5. "Miami's New Cubans," *Newsweek International*, January 18, 1999, www.newsweek.com/nw~srv/printed/int/wa/ovin0103_4.htm, February 2, 1999.

6. E-mail from Peter Sánchez, April 12, 1999.

Epilogue

1. Quoted by González-Pando, *The Cuban Americans*, ix.

2. Boswell and Curtis, *The Cuban-American Experience*, 158.

3. Anonymous quote to authors, April 10, 1999.

About the Authors

Robert M. Levine is the Gabelli Senior Scholar of Arts and Sciences and director of Latin American studies at the University of Miami. He has published two dozen books, including several titles on Cuba.

Moisés Asís is a Cuban American scientist and lawyer, who has published fourteen books. He has served as an investigator for the Florida Department of Children and Families, and as executive director of the Dante B. Fascell Center for Conflict Resolution and Peace.